T0129897

FORGOTTEN PIECES

FORGOTTEN PIECES

A LIFE SKILLS GUIDE FOR TEENS AND YOUNG ADULTS

MONIQUE DONYALE

FORGOTTEN PIECES
A LIFE SKILLS GUIDE FOR TEENS

iUniverse books may be ordered through booksellers or by contacting:

iUniverse
1663 Liberty Drive
Bloomington, IN 47403
www.iuniverse.com
1-800-Authors (1-800-288-4677)

Monique Donyale Publishing
Willingboro, NJ
(888) 677-6129
www.moniquedonyalepublishing.com

ISBN: 978-1-5320-2088-9 (sc)
ISBN: 978-1-5320-2045-2 (e)

Library of Congress Control Number: 2017904682

Print information available on the last page.

iUniverse rev. date: 04/05/2017

CONTENTS

Chapter 1   Goal Setting 1

Chapter 2   Time Management 10

Chapter 3   Learning Styles and Study Skills 16

Chapter 4   Self-Esteem 25

Chapter 5   Bullying 29

Chapter 6   How to Develop Good Communication
and Social Skills 35

Chapter 7   Job vs Career 40

Chapter 8   Seek And Maintain Employment 52

Chapter 9   Money Matters 62

Chapter 10 Investing 74

Chapter 11 Credit 86

Chapter 12 Paying Taxes 100

Chapter 13 Apartment Rental 103

Chapter 14 Purchasing a Home 118

Chapter 15 Purchasing a Car 123

Chapter 16 Food and Exercise 130

Chapter 17 Hygiene Tips 136

Chapter 18 Beauty Budget 141

Chapter 19 Mentors and Spiritual Advisers 149

Chapter 20 Empowering Parents 153

Chapter 21 The Power of "I Am" 163

ACKNOWLEDEMENTS

I would like to thank everyone who put their heart
and soul into helping me complete this book

Styling team @ Monique Donyale Dominican Salon located in Willingboro NJ call 856-677-6047 for more information on the latest hair styling & appointments. We are open 7 days for your convenience. MoniqueDonyaleDominicanSalon.com Like us on FB

Cosmetic team @ Monique Donyale Collection located in the salon also on line at MoniqueDonyaleCollection.com This collection consist of Skin Care, Make up, 100% human hair bundles, Hair care products and a boutique.

Photographers- Taunya Sills front and back cover shots of Monique Donyale and some inside shots. Contact info; Image by Taunya Sills Photography 240-232-5981,Maryland

Photographer-Sean Dylan Perry - some inside shots. Contact info perry.dylan.sean@gmail.com California

Photographer-Jeffrey Johnson- cover shot for Champayne. Contact info Jeffrey.johnson@nyfa.edu California

Cover shot-Monique Donyale & Champayne Marte make up and wardrobe was done using the Monique Donyale Make up Collection & on line boutique

My beautiful & talented daughter Champayne Marte- setting up the on line boutique and helping me to see the world from a young adult perspective which became my motivation to write this book.

All of the people who did the photo shoot for this book: Champayne Marte, Sean Perry, Stefan Leach, Taunya Siles, Thomas Orr 3rd, Keisha Orr, Nasyah Orr, Bayani Orr, Tawana Flowers, Kavon E. Pugh, Judea Robinson, Adrian Singleton, James Singleton, Jadeb Singleton, Rochelle Gray, Caity Gray

BOOK- DEDICATIONS

Giving honor to GOD first, who is the head of my life. God is our anchor in the times of the storm. "For God did not give us a spirit of fear, but he has given us a spirit of power, and of love, and of calm and a well-balanced mine, discipline and self-control."

Writing and completing this book has been a journey that has answered some of the questions that I have asked GOD through-out my life. What is my Divine purpose? What was I born to do? I knew what my goals where but I was still unclear about my Divine Purpose. Now I am clear. A divine purpose is based on intention. By being who you are, you live your divine purpose in every moment through every situation you encounter. Life Skills and wisdom will show you who the Boss is although every experience offers the opportunity for you to become more authentically you. Manifesting your divine purpose is not driven by job titles but is motivated by your inner strength to do better and help others do better. I now know that I can achieve my divine purpose by becoming a living, breathing expression of divinity in everything I do. My Divine Purpose is to teach people that "BEAUTY START WITHIN" through self-empowerment and awareness of who you are meant to be.

I dedicate this book to my daughter Champayne (Princess Cham) Monique Marte who has given me unbelievable strength and determination to always do better because our well-being depends on it. Champayne is smart, ambitious, assertive, creative, focused, beautiful and an awesome daughter. I am so very proud to be your mom. You want to be an actress and I will always pray for that dream for you and hold your hand until you walk on your own. Mommy loves you very much and thanks you for loving me back. I am your number one fan.

To my immediate family for believing in me and always supporting all of my business ventures, I love you very much-My grandmother Florence Singleton(R.I.P), My mom Dina Robinson, my stepfather Larry Robinson, brother Larry (Quan) McKever, sister Shantica (Shay) Robinson, sister Brianna(Beya) Robinson, Sister Ebony(Ebby) Robinson, brother Judea(Ju Ju) Robinson, brother Keith Wright, niece Tatyana(Princess Tot) Mckever, nephew Laquan(Quanny) McKever, nephew John(Jack) Dwyer, nephew Devon(Tuda) Chavis and niece Nilah(Aunty niece) McKever

To my dad Bobby Horton for all the advice that you gave me about Men and the long talks of encouragement. May you rest in peace. I will always love you.

To my step kids for loving me through all my life changes and still including me in your life. Alicia Marte(my daughter) (granddaughters Ja'Lysa Grant & Haidyn Zarina) Rene(Tony) Marte 3rd(my son) and Allan Casso(my son)

To my cousins for all the encouraging talks and guidance that you have given me through- out my life's mission no matter what the emergency. Cheryl (Wakia) Lewis, Cathy Shivers, Pam Lewis, Charlotte (kydedra) Lewis, Hashec Lewis, Trisha Orr, Vanessa Orr, Raheem Orr, Robin Orr, Taliek Wise, Tawana Flowers, Thomas Orr 3rd, & his wife Keisha Orr, Michelle Sessoms, Uncle Paul, Aunt Lee, Aunt Earlene and Angela (Angy) Williams

To my cousin Stacey Lamont Williams (Shadee) and two of my dearest friends Gregory Wonguist and Darren Dowdy, I want to thank you for the emotional and financial support that you have always given me. Words can't describe the male leadership roles that you have played in my life.

To my lifelong friends, words can't describe your untimely dedication and devotion in my life. Timothy Jones(R.I.P),Sidney Harrison Jr (R.I.P), Joey Johnson, Marixsa Rolon, Reggie Sumner, James Womack, Donna Stringer,

Cecelia Bethea, Larry McKever Senior, Henry Murry, Kenneth Thomas, Esq, Rochelle Gray, Deborah Smith Simpkins, Bob Mark Walston, Mike Burwell, Taunya Sills, Kason Hazzard, Ruby Shivers, Ruben Price, Kim Solomon, Prentiss Thompson, Tina Graham, Bob Sumner, Steve McGill, Frances(Tiny)Billie and Jilma Bell-Beecham.

To my Godmothers who have always advised me and lent a helping hand. Your love has helped mold me into the Lady I am today. Johnnie Mae Lewis and Evelyn Rolon

To my spiritual advisers for all the prayers and keeping me focused on the higher power. Prophet Beatty, CP Lacy and Heather Walker

To iUniverse for all your support in editing and distributing my book. Your company has helped me through a challenging process by working diligently with me at all times.

I would just like to thank everyone that have played a significant part in my life whether you have helped me or tried to hinder me; my divine purpose will be my legacy.

INTRODUCTION

It is my intention to facilitate positive change in others, so that they engage in the life-skills process with greater passion and less self-doubt. In doing so, my hope is to help educate and guide the transformation from the teen years to a young adult a more peaceful, balanced and positive experience. My name is Monique Donyale, from Elizabeth NJ. After graduating from Elizabeth High School, I attended Hampton University in Virginia then Wilfred Academy in Newark NJ. I am an entrepreneur and have been for 26 years. I am the founder of Monique Donyale Productions and Champayne Enterprizes(a real estate investment company). Under my production company I ventured into many projects such as owning 6 hair salons, The Monique Donyale Show(a live internet radio show), Monique Donyale Collection(on-line business selling my brand of skin care, make up, hair extensions, hair care products & a boutique) modeling camps, motivational speaking and self publishing this, book through Monique Donyale Publishing. This book is based on my thoughts of what teenagers and young adults need to be equipped with before they embark in this game called LIFE. This is not a dress rehearsal. I hope this book will serve as a guideline that you can refer to throw out your life.

My family consisted of a mom and stepfather and five siblings, who I am the oldest. I have a beautiful daughter named Champayne. My life wasn't easy and being the oldest you had no choice but to learn life skills at an early age from the school of hard Knox. Helping get my brother and sisters ready for school, making small meals, going to the Laundromat and helping with homework is a life that I know all to well. Those experiences are one of the reasons that I am writing this book today. Sometimes parents are so busy working two jobs, hanging out or learning themselves that they get lost in life and send their children to face the world unprepared.

There is an emotional toll to entering adulthood unprepared. As exciting as it is to be out on one's own it can be scary, lonely and frustrating. Saving for essentials like rent, food, clothes, and transportation can be overwhelming in the beginning to have the entire burden suddenly place on their own shoulders. For the first time in their lives, young adults who find themselves juggling adult responsibilities can feel lonely, anxious and fearful. Insecurity can lead to depression, poor decision making, impulsive choices, career stagnation and even health problems.

You are the master of your plan, I am here to help facilitate that plan, guide you to greater fulfillment and help you discover tools that empower you and help you reach your goals. Consciously embracing both your individual mission and your Divine Purpose will allow you to be you and help you get real with the issues in your life.

More often than not 9-12 grade students leave home without learning about life skills because their parents do everything for them. We think that we are helping them by giving them less responsibility, eliminating choirs or helping out with dinner but we are just being enablers. Parents use excuses like they are so spoiled or their homework comes first. This may be true but there is a limit too the foolishness. As we all know teenagers and young adults have a THINKING ERROR, there sense of entitlement leads them down the wrong path causing major disasters. A THINKING ERROR is just like making a spelling error, if you don't correct the mistake it will happen over and over again.

There are major hurdles to overcome in life. It's not like using a navigation system when your lost you can just put in your starting point and end up at your destination. You have to work at LIFE. One such hurdle for me was impulse shopping, like anything else such as over eating or smoking cigarettes when your depressed, impulse shopping can be dangerous. Strict management of needs versus wants is crucial when just starting out on one's own. It is not uncommon for young people to make unsound decisions that they grow to regret just because they want something. "Why did I spend $150 on sneakers when I had a car insurance payment due?" Or worse, "I signed a one year lease for a very expensive apartment to impress my friends, and now I can't pay the rent." We don't want our young adults making foolish decision that they will grow to regret based on their wants. I'm telling you what I know, not what I heard. Young adults must learn how to delay gratification because reality will show them that they must work hard to take care of their needs before they can have what they want. You will get out of life what you put in.

In this book I will discuss life-skills such as goal setting, organizational skills, time management, transitioning from middle-high school to college or trade school, self esteem, communication and social skills, job vs careers, budgeting your monthly bills, why your credit is important tips on how to get hired, moving out on your own, how to do healthy food shopping while in college, fashion budgeting while broke and fabulous, how to buy and maintain it, why having a mentor is important, how to be a winner and assist you in finding your DEVINE PURPOSE.

Throughout this life skills guide, I will challenge teens and young adults to examine their judgments and interpretations, Encourage them to think and reflect about their feelings, To have more confidence, to create and sustain healthier relationships, To be more motivated, to have more energy, to be happier and more positive about life, I will be HONEST with you and Remind you that you are destined for greatness!

I hope that this guide will take away some of the anxiety of becoming an AWESOME and INDEPENDENT adult.

Chapter 1

Goal Setting

Dream Big- Who are you and who do you want to be???

Life totally depends on how you set your goals. This is one of the most Thought out LIFE SKILL. I'm sure we have all asked ourselves, what do I want to be when I grow up? This thought pattern can be pretty scary when asked in high school, especially when you're trying to figure out what sports or clubs you may want to join that year. Setting Smart goals is a success strategy children can learn at an early age. Creating a plan and identifying skills students need to improve could have a significant impact on a student's academic growth. Evaluating, daily, weekly and yearly goals can help you break down the overwhelming stress of overseeing your life. Goal setting is MANDATORY. "If life is a journey, how will you get there if you don't have an itinerary? Goals tell you where you are going, how you are going to get there, and what you will do when you get there".

Decide what you want. Goal setting is the opposite of floating through life letting things happen to you. If you don't know what you want to achieve and succeed at in life, then you risk being open to doing whatever others suggest. Setting goals requires you to make a decision about what you actually want. It helps you shift through your strong and week points. Striving for goals lets you achieve your known desires. Goal setting requires setting a deadline, so that you don't waste precious time.

1

Evaluating Goals

The Who, What, When, Where, Why and How Goals help the student think through various aspects of the chosen goal and how it will be achieved. This style of goal setting is great at developing the student's self-awareness as to why the goal is important to her and better defines a strategy to accomplish the goal.

Daily Goals

Setting daily goals may include the smaller steps required by larger or long-term goals. Daily goal Setting requires the student to evaluate himself on a daily basis as to how well he performed in meeting his goals. Daily evaluation serves as an intervention to limit procrastination and the development of bad habits that interfere with successful goal accomplishments.

Weekly Goals

Setting weekly goals require you to match your goals to relevant areas of life. It's not unusual to have general goals that apply to all areas of your life. Things like, "I want to be successful", or "I want to be rich". They're aspirations with broad intent rather than specific road maps. By detailing your goals into specific realms of your life, you'll gain more control and sense of purpose over them. Assign your goals to different aspects of your life. Perhaps have one or two goals for each area to begin with. These areas might include: school, career and social. For example, If you say, "I want to pass my History exam this week, then set aside a specific amount of time each day to study until the day of the exam

Yearly Goals

These goals are set to show your yearly growth and accomplishments. Habituate yourself to liking the challenges. The most difficult thing is to *like* something useful. Many people focus subconsciously on the petty, shallow things in life, such as entertainment, being the next Michael Jordan, celebrity-watching, wishing after the lifestyles of the rich and famous, etc., and when time comes for focusing on big goals for ourselves, we back out because we see it as beyond our own capabilities. It is simply misinterpreted reality. There is reason to feel worthless before a big goal just because you have liked petty goals. Substitute the shallow with thinking big when you're setting goals––allow yourself to think great thoughts.

Review your progress. After setting, affirming and doing, comes reviewing. As part of setting your goals, be sure to write in occasional statements requiring you to "review this goal's progress". It's an important reminder to keep you on the path of achieving the goals you've set for yourself. Now go set your goals and start working on them!

Stay on your path to your goals

☐ Be realistic in setting your R.E.A.D.Y Goals, and in achieving them. Give yourself a break if needed—go for a walk, stand up and move, eat a snack.

☐ Remember to advocate for yourself! If you need help, do ask for it!

☐ Review your READY Goals and remind yourself how important your goal is to you.

Try the worksheet below to get you started on setting READY Goals

To be successful, goals should be READY:

☐ **Realistic** – You must be able to visualize yourself in that position

☐ **Exciting** – Your goal must be specific and in-line with your dreams

☐ **Achievable**- This is something you can see happening in the near future

☐ **Daily**- Setting daily goals may include the smaller steps required by larger or long-term goals

☐ **Yearly**- Goals should have beginning and ending dates.

READY GOAL WORKSHEET

1. Write the goal you want to achieve at the top of your paper. State your goal in one or two sentences. Make sure that you write down obtainable goals first.
2. Write down in two or three sentences why this goal is important to you.
3. Write a date by which you want to achieve your goal.
4. List each specific step you will need to take to reach your goal. Decide which step you will have to complete first, which step second, third, etc., and list them in that order.
5. List all the resources you will need to reach your goal.
6. List people who you know will encourage you in reaching your goal. Under each name, write down how and when you will contact this person about your goal. I call it a SMART TEAM.

7. List the top three roadblocks or difficulties you anticipate encountering while working toward your goal. For each difficulty or roadblock, list ideas of how you would deal with it. Your SMART TEAM should enforce tough love to help you get through this phase.
8. Look over your worksheet. Evaluate how realistic your plan is and make any adjustments needed. It's OK to have long term goals of even a three year projection, but don't confuse that with your right now goals.

Let's take a look at a goal. Is it READY?

"Beginning this month, I will save $75 a month until I have enough money in a savings account to pay for two months' rent."

Ask yourself;

Is it Realistic, Exciting, Achievable?

Can I break this down to saving DAILY? Ex. divide $75 by the days in a month

How much would I have if I continued to save this amount YEARLY?

Activity

Now that you know about READY goals, think about your own goals. Which goals are short-term and which are long-term? Write them down on a piece of paper and put them somewhere in your room so you can see them daily. I usually hang it on my bedroom wall by my closet. When you accomplish a goal, reward yourself on a job well done! No matter how big or small. It will make you proud and motivated.

Examples of READY Goals in Education

Another example of a READY Goal is choosing a career with good FINANCIAL STABILITY. It's no secret that many college students pursue a degree in higher education to ensure that their future will be financially secure. While a college degree doesn't guarantee a fiscally fruitful career, study in certain fields, such as engineering and computer science, can increase the likelihood of bigger paychecks. Studying business administration can provide the skills, connections and experience necessary to generate a large income in the entrepreneur and corporate world. To make financial stability a primary educational goal, it's smart to pick fields in areas with starting salaries no lower than $40,000.

What are Organizational Skills?

Once you decide to do something, there will always be speed bumps in the road to slow you down. You have to keep a positive mind set to be successful. When you decide to pursue your career, you must be prepared to face difficult challenges. Being in the business world can be awesome but you need to cultivate some skills to achieve your career goals. One of these skills would be Organizational Skills... It might be quite challenging to do it at first but as time passes, you will be able to master your organizational skills. You will no longer find it hard to organize yourself and be more successful with your work.

ADVANTAGES OF USING ORGANIZATIONAL SKILLS

Here are 6 tips to help you develop your organizational skills:

1. Self motivation
Improve your organizational skills and try to be more disciplined in whatever you are doing. Determine what went wrong with it and do something to answer the problem.

2. Have self-discipline.
Having self-discipline is the primary key to be organized. It really takes an effort for some people in order to achieve organizational skills. You have to see to it that you really do things in order to keep organized. Force yourself to organize your school work, to clean your area, to make a to-do-list and others. This will be your starting point. Soon, you won't need to force yourself, it will only come out naturally once you got used to it

3. Prioritize

It is important that you learn to prioritize for you to make sure that the most important tasks are done first. Everything does not have to be done at the same time. Being able to prioritize is part of organizational skills. Even if you have made a list already and have acquired effective tools for organizing stuff, you will still fail if you were not able to prioritize.

4. Get ready the night before

You will save yourself time if you get everything you need and put it in a safe place near the door the night before. Also knowing what you are going to wear the night before saves alot of miss used time in the morning.

5. Good work output

Reducing clutter in your area is one sign that you have achieved organizational skills. Make it a habit to clean your area before and after work. Keep unnecessary things away and arrange things properly. File your papers, dispose things you no longer need, throw away unnecessary papers, organize your files in the computer and do other things to make your work area free of clutter.

6. Start small

You have to start small so you won't become overwhelmed when developing your organizational skills. Do not jump into a big task for it will only discourage you. The project will seem unattainable and you will talk yourself out of the job. So, start small by listing what needs to be done first and so on. Do little by little. For example you can start with your room and then your homework.

4 DISADVANTAGES OF POOR ORGANIZATONAL SKILLS

Many people want to advance their careers or be an entrepreneur. The business world is fast-paced and always forward bound. To keep up with industrial growth and your own personal advancement, it's essential to practice good organizational skills. Disorganization can cause you to confuse dates, mix up assignments, and miss deadlines and, in turn, this makes you unreliable and undependable. Some careers--such as an entrepreneur -require good organizational skills to form a pro active team.

When a position calls for an employee to be orderly, but they cannot exhibit signs of good organizational skills, it can result in the employee being dismissed from a project or terminated from their position.

☐ Unreliable

Poor organizational skills make people less efficient and unreliable in school and in the business world. Those two qualities do not work well in either situation am a Boss and to make my Brand successful, my team need to be dependable, eager to learn and reliable for us to succeed. When it comes to school you must work well with others on projects and joint ventures to increase your productivity in the outside world. Being unreliable or making excuses for your laziness will only get you frustrated, fired and a low GPA.

☐ Poor work ethics

Working in an environment that is neat and tidy will increase your ability to get things done. If you are the type of person that arrives at school or work just before your time or don't organize your day the night before, I'm talking to you. You have poor work ethics. When you arrive early there is time to go over your TO DO LIST that was written the night before and reduces time wasted on getting your work started. Having poor work ethics shows that you are not that interested in your career choice and may need to choose another path to your success. When you enjoy your career its not work it's a life style.

☐ Poor Time Management Skills

Poor time management skills influences your ability to manage your time well. This has a tendency to result in a failure to prioritize assignments, complete projects on time and prepare you for your destiny in life. Stop wasting your time on nonsense that has nothing to do with preparing your future. Its OK to goof off sometimes but don't spend your life in a RUTT. Decide who you want to be and schedule your time around positive people that will encourage your growth. Stop entertaining people that are dream killers. What God has for you, is for you. Start managing your time like your life depends on it. Life is not a dress rehearsal so stop acting and get to being the best you possible by managing your time better.

☐ Effects on Health

There is definitely a link between organizational skills and your mental and physical health. When I am working on a new venture and i don't know what the future holds, i tend you have anxiety and stress. Not because i think I'm gonna fail but because i may win. What if God is opening up the door or window and it is time for me to fly. I have spent so much time organizing my goals that i didn't plan my exit strategy from my old life to my new life. This can be pretty scary and cause headaches and anxiety. For example;you have spent 12 years working on your plan to graduate high school but you forgot to create your exit plan to your new life as a young adult or you studied so hard to past the supervisors test but forgot to plan your exit strategy to your new life as a boss. All I'm saying is whether you win or loose, how you view your life will have an effect on your health but always stay positive and you will prevail

To sum it all up, Goal Setting and Organizational skills go hand in hand. Master these two skills and you will be on top of your game sooner than later. Use your SMART TEAM to keep you focused. Life is not a dress rehearsal so stop acting and get to being the best you possible.

CHAPTER 2

WHAT IS TIME MANAGEMENT?

Life Skills is all about how you manage your time. Time management is the act or process of planning and exercising conscious control over the amount of time spent on specific activities, especially to increase effectiveness, efficiency or productivity. Time Management will teach you how to be the boss of your life. Displaying time management will take away your self doubt because you have an agenda and managing your time will be your navigation to positive results. Everything need not be done in one day. Do the most important things first and the least effective things last. Remember you have 7 days in a weak, if you plan accordingly you can schedule one-two days off for family time and friends.

Time Management includes:

☐ **Being punctual and disciplined**
Plan your day well in advance. Prepare a To Do List" preferably the night before. If you wake up and you know what to expect of yourself that day, it will make it easier to work. Be 15 minutes early, allot time for your coffee or tea before your work day start or just have 15 minutes to talk to God and get your armor on to fight the enemy with ease. I promise you that being punctual and discipline will make your fears become a challenge instead of a road block

☐ **Setting Goals and Objectives**

Working without goals and targets would be similar to not having your GPS to navigate to unknown places. Goals and objectives are our navigation through life, the only difference is in life we can't see the end result but we can plan to succeed. Set targets for yourself and make sure they are realistic ones and achievable.

☐ **Build character**

Learn to take ownership of work. One person who can best set the deadlines is you yourself. Take control of your life right from the start. Learn about who you are and where you come from. You will make mistakes but embrace them, forgive yourself and stay in the race. Others will always try to remind you of your failures but don't fold. Be aggressive and assertive. Don't take NO for an answer. Life is yours, if you OWN IT.

☐ **Setting deadline**

Learn to say "NO" at school or at the workplace. Don't take on more than you can handle by fooling yourself into thinking that nobody else can do the job. The truth is other people can do the job you where just more prepared to take the position. Learn to delegate responsibilities according to other people strong points. Set a deadline and stick to it no matter what. Learning to appreciate people for there time and work will always equal to a job well done on time.

☐ **Delegation of responsibilities**

Prioritize the tasks as per their importance and urgency. Know the difference between important and urgent work. Work done at the wrong time is not of much use. Don't waste a complete day on something which can be done in an hour or so. Also keep some time separate for your personal calls or checking updates on Facebook, linked in, Instagram, face time and Twitter. After all you are a human being and all work and no play stinks.

I guess you can see now that goal setting, organizational skills and time management all work together for a more productive life. First set your goal, follow through with organizing them and finally set aside the appropriate time to complete them. Time Management helps an individual to adopt a planned approach in life.

Factors that affect Time Management

- ☐ **Not scheduling in enough time for Family and friends,** Relationships, Recreation Other commitments (church, PTO, organizations, work-out schedule etc…) You must allow enough time for these activities

- ☐ **Not Setting READY goals**. Goal setting can help motivate us to do better. Goals must be higher enough to motivate us, but not too high to set us up for failure.

- ☐ **Not Maintaining a Balance"** – Healthy mind and a healthy body. A balance in the amount of activity and relaxation is very important. Never sacrifice sleep as a way to add more time in your schedule

- ☐ **Distractions!** Examine what things tend to distract you from completing things you need to complete; examples: phone, TV, siblings, friends… Come up with strategies to avoid or eliminate those distractions Do not schedule study time during your favorite TV show, or when you friend is coming over etc…

- ☐ **Not organizing you, punctuality and meeting deadlines**. Be on time so you will not miss important information. Important dates for test and assignments are often made the first few minutes of the class. Hand in work and assignments on time. School is your job – late employees get fired and late students fail. Choose a place to study and do assignment that is conducive to learning and studying. Have all of the supplies you will need handy. Lead a healthy lifestyle. Healthy diet feeds your brain, while sleep replenishes your brain.

- ☐ **Not understanding the assignment and instructions thoroughly.** Understand the grading system completely and how the assignment will be evaluated. Decide what kind of information will be needed. Be able to identify sources to help you with the assignment. Gather and obtain all of the information you will need. Document sources if needed. Create a rough outline or draft of the assignment. Make corrections to the assignment. Check your assignment for any mistakes, make sure you have followed directions and that everything needed is included. Hand the assignment in on time

TIME MANAGEMENT METHOD

How do I use the Monique Donyale method for time management? Here are 4 easy steps

☐ Write out your daily to-do list the night before. Write everything you want to accomplish.

☐ Label each task 1,2,3 for errands and A, B, C etc. for phone calling jobs

☐ The numbed items are jobs that you need to do in person, #1 being the most important. The lettered items are phone calls to be made, letter A being the most important.

☐ Schedule time for all of the phone calls first, then get moving on all the in person stops to be made that day. Remember if you have an appointment always set aside the proper traveling time so that you are not late or get road rage.

Refer to your list to keep you focused and on track.

Time Management Skills

☐ **Be a good listener**—Don't be so quick to claim to know everything. Listen to what other people have to say, you just might learn something that may help you succeed.

☐ **Communicate-** your way is not always the best or more practical way. There is more than one way to skin a cat. Ask other people do they have any ideas about the subject at hand. Take what you need and use it to your advantage. Communication helps you to find other ways to complete a task

☐ **Be 15 mins early**—Don't leave with just enough time to arrive at your destination and dash in the building. This will cause road rage and disappointment because other people could care less about your lack of time management. Arriving early gives you the upper hand on your work day and allows you to finish first.

☐ **Avoid gossiping**—use positive reinforcement to motivate yourself. Sitting around gossiping about love and hip hop or checking your Snap Chat is not putting money in your pocket. There is a time and place for everything and the work place is not designed to cater to foolishness so stay focused and make some money

- ☐ **Stick to your schedule**—Monitor your attitude and behavior. Track your accomplishments. Don't rearrange your schedule of importance to appease other people who are not helping you strive in life. You are your best friend so take control of your destiny.
- ☐ **Study difficult or boring subjects first**-. If a task seems hard, get started. Half the battle is beginning. Be aware of your best time of day—study when you'll be alert.
- ☐ **Use waiting time** (study note cards while on the bus or standing in line)
- ☐ **Use a regular study area or a library**-Avoid scheduling marathon study sessions. You will only regret that you have to finish. Don't be to hard on yourself
- ☐ **Pay attention to your attention**—are you focusing? Learn to say no. Notice how you misuse your time and change your habits. Coordinate with roommates or family members about study time.

What can I do to avoid being a procrastinator?

<u>**Procrastination:**</u> Putting off work, postponing decisions, and not starting or finishing tasks are all forms of procrastination.

Activity

Are you wasting time procrastinating instead of stepping into your destiny?

How many hours do you sleep a day?

How many hours do you spend with your friends?

How many hours do you spend with your boyfriend/girlfriend?

How many hours a day do you spend on personal grooming (hair, make up, nails)?

How much time do you spend at work/school?

How many hours are spent on errands?

How many hours do you spend texting and on the phone?

How many hours do you spend studying?

Other activities?

There are only 24 hours in a day, use your time wisely. Life is yours if you OWN IT!!!!

Chapter 3

In This Chapter We Will Focus on Learning Styles & Studying Skills and How They Relate to Life Skills

What is a learning style and why is it important to identify yours?

Learning styles are simply different approaches or ways of learning. Your learning style can ultimately improve your grades. Figuring out your learning style will help identify what strategies to use to fit your learning abilities. Everybody has a preferred learning style. Knowing and understanding our learning style helps us to learn more effectively. Through identifying your learning style, you will be able to capitalize on your strengths and improve your life skills.

The 7 Learning styles

Visual- You prefer using pictures, images, diagrams, colors and maps to move around life. You can visualize places before you arrive and you will very seldom ask for directions or get lost.

A visual learner may use phases like"'SEE HOW THIS WORKS FOR YOU" or I NEVER FORGET A FACE"

Aural -You prefer using sound, music, recordings and rhymes. It's like music to your ears. You will most likely be in a band, hum tunes and notice the back round music in movies, commercials and other media.

An Aural leaner may use phases like "THAT SOUNDS ABOUT RIGHT" or "THATS MUSIC TO MY EARS"

Verbal- You prefer using words, both in speech and writing to assist in learning. You can appreciate using new words and knowing their meaning when communicating with others. Because you know the meaning of many words, you have fun with reading and writing.

A verbal learner may use phases like "LETS TALK LATER" or "LET ME SPELL IT OUT FOR YOU"

Physical- You learn by using the body, hands and sense of touch. You like to get up and move around. Exercise, sports and gardening is right up your ally. Sitting down in lectures or meeting to long will drive you crazy. You feel comfortable using body language and planning your day in your head while exercising. Going for a long drive or a run always make you feel better when you are troubled or upset.

A physical learner may use phases like "I CANT GET A GRIP ON THIS" or "MY GUT IS TELLING ME"

Logical-You prefer using logic and have a good ability to understand the bigger picture. You like creating agendas, itineraries and to do list in numerical order as a plan of action to stay focused and have a productive day. You classify and group information to help you process and learn it better. You are also good with numbers and putting budgets in place that can be tracked so you can see your progress

A Logical learner may use phases like "WE CAN WORK IT OUT" or "PROVE IT"

Social- You prefer to learn in groups or with other people as much as possible. You communicate well verbally and non-verbal. People may come to you for advise often because you listen well and are compassionate toward others. You may be a good counselor or mentor. You like to learn in groups and prefer social activities instead of doing your own thing.

A Social learner may use phases such as "LET'S WORK TOGETHER ON THIS or "TELL ME WHAT YOU ARE THINKING"

Solitary- You prefer to work alone and use self study. You feel you know yourself well and like spending time alone. You will more than likely be self employed. You think independently and if you don't know your current direction in life you are not satified and unhappy. You like to set plans and goals. You are private and focus well on your current situation and the direction that you need to take to better your plan.

A Solitary learner may use phases like "I WOULD LIKE TIME TO THINK ON THAT or I'LL GET BACK TO YOU"

Understanding the basis of the learning styles.

Although there are 7 learning styles, we have broken them down to really only using three; visual, physical and audible. In reality a combination of multiple learning styles help solidify the learning that takes place. If you are a teacher, i have studied that combining study skills is an effective way to make your learning stick.

There are alot of on line test you can take to determine your learning style

What are Study Skills?

Study Skills are important because it is a transferable set
of life skills that will help you to study and learn.

Everybody learns differently, there is know right or wrong way. Whether you are a student or not, you have to develop how to learn. You have to know the concept and idea of what you are trying to learn. Once you learn what works for you, study skills will help you throughout your life.

Once you learn how to study, you will be unstoppable. Study Skills will help with goal setting, time management and all the important disciplinary measures you need to be focused and well diversed in any area of life that you stumble upon to keep you motivated.

Finding a location to study is a good Study Skill

There is know good or bad location. Its all up to your learning style. You may like to study in a crowded room with the TV and radio on but i may like a cubicle with no noise. Find what works for you and stick with it.

When studying it is important to find a comfortable location

This may not seem important but studying in an uncomfortable position can be distracting and you will spend more time trying to find a comfortable position than studying. It's also a good idea to make sure that you have all the materials needed to complete your work. Getting up looking for pens, paper or other material will just delay the process of finishing your work. Studying also require good lighting. Just because you are in a comfortable location doesn't mean the lighting is appropriate. Good lighting and a comfortable location are both necessary when practicing good study habits.

Set a Routine

It is important to choose the same time and location when studying. This will get you pre ready before you actually start studying. It will help to prepare your mind for the task ahead. Be careful not to pick a location that is distracting no matter what your study preference is. For example if you like to listen to the radio, don't study in a place where the radio is on your favorite station because you will find yourself humming every song and not focusing on your work.

Set study rules

When studying it is important to set rules for yourself just like you have rules in everyday life. Rules help keep you focused and on a schedule. Set rules like, I will study for an hour and then take a 15 minute break. Taking a break will give your brain a rest and help you to retain information better once you resume your work. Let friends and family know that during these hours you will be studying and please do not distract you with nonsense. Having good role models around you will help to increase your study habits and make your studying time more productive.

Take good notes

Effective note taking is very important key to succeeding in school or college. It is very common to not retain important information hurd in class. If you have legible notes you can always refer back and learn the key elements to pass your class. Even the smartest people have trouble remembering major dates, times and events without studying their notes. Comparing notes with classmates is also a good idea because you may have missed a vital piece of information that might be on the test. This rule applies for any test that you take in life, don't be afraid to get a study group together and brainstorm, it may be the difference in a pass or fail grade.

Come to class prepared by reviewing your notes the night before. This will help you develop questions to ask your teacher or professor that you don't understand. Surround yourself with like minded people, don't sit around other students that will be distracting by laughing, giggling or playing around. Make your education a priority not a plan B.

Organizing your notes, using abbreviations and writing clearly are all signs of good note taking. Start by organizing your notes with the subject, class and date at the top. Keep each subject separate. Abbreviations will help you write down more thoughts because it is challenging to write full sentences when someone is talking a mile a minute. Always write clear because there is nothing like trying to review your notes and realizing that you can't even understand your own chicken scratch. Now all of that hard work was for nothing. It is also a good idea when in college to use a tape recording device and write your notes at home if you are that disciplined to follow up.

Improve your reading comprehension

Reading comprehension skills are necessary to have a successful adult career and is imperative to excelling academically. It doesn't matter if you are the fastest reader or the slowest reader in your class or surroundings, if you do not understand what you have read, you are still lost.

To get a better understanding of what you read skim through the chapter or book first. Read the introduction, the outline and chapter headings first. Always keep your yellow highlighter handy so that you can stay focused on general information not specifics. This will also help you focus and find direction.

Set a goal when you are reading a paragraph, chapter or book. Ask yourself what am i trying to learn. Be specific and remember when you learned how to write an essay you where taught that the first paragraph is what the entire essay will explain, well it's the same thing except you are breaking it down to smaller focus points. Next read the subtitles before each section in bold print, again they will provide basic focus points and help you navigate through your work with a better understanding. Now here is where it gets interesting. The first sentence in the paragraph will provide the main thought but sometimes it's just an attention getter so you should read the first and second sentence to get an idea of the major themes to look for.

In reading comprehension the summary and study questions will always give you a summary of what you just read. This my friend will help you to define all of the important information that you should have retained during your studies.

Identifying what you have learned will help you recognize the material that you did not retain, so you can spend the proper amount of time on material that you need work on.

Improving your memory is definitely a study skill to practice

When it come to remembering, some things are easier than others. You will not retain information that you cannot relate to. If you don't break it down into what you understand it will be useless.

Categorize information, if you are studying to be a fireman and a school teacher you cannot study them together because they are very different careers. What you would do is put each different career into its category, then itemize it by compartments until you have small segment based on functions or location and study each career separately.

Associating something new with something that you are already familiar with will help you remember it better. This works well with learning new vocabulary words because it helps the brain to learn and remember the unfamiliar. Story telling is another memory exercise that works well. When you relate an event to a story your brain remembers it because one event will triggers the next event and before you know it, your memory is endless. A lot of actors may use this concept to remember scripts.

Talking about time, date and places can be important to your memory because the more you talk about something, the more you retain it. Want to learn about a subject then talk to someone who already know that subject. Through dialogue or debate you will remember specific things that are important and will be helpful later.

Many people use Mnemonic devices to remember specific details from readings or lecturers. This method is very helpful because you relate facts with short phrases or anything that rhymes or that you are familiar with together to remember it. For example if a definition to a word starts with M which is my first initial by remembering the definition starts with M will trigger the first word and it will help me to remember the definition. Another example of the Mnemonic system is to use acronyms such as IHOP which means the International House of Pancakes.

If you never want to forget anything, put it to a familiar song or music and you will remember it 20 years from now. There is something about music and catchy tunes that stick with you. I sometimes find myself humming songs i don't even like because of the beat. Try it, you won't go wrong.

Improving your memory is a very powerful tool that will help you with your life skills

Learning information has a lot to do with Effective listening skills

Many students and adults go through life hearing and not listening. Effective listening helps you to process the information given to you. Before you enter into a conversation or lecture make sure that you have the central idea of what the message is about and are you getting the important details. Don't retain everything, just learn what makes sense in the content of the topic. At the end of the topic make sure that you understood what was being communicated to you. If you don't understand then ask questions. Even if it's challenging information through good note taking and effective listening you can always create questions to ask later.

Learn how to focus and concentrate on what is being said to you. Stop worrying about what your friends are doing or what bills are do next week. If you can not concentrate you will not be a good listener. Don't worry about things that are out of your control. Be prepared, learn the backround knowledge of being a good student, adult and listener. Focus on what is important. People who matter care and people who care matter. It is a mistake to only be concerned with the facts, learn the story behind the facts and then you can pick up on the main topics and concepts behind the facts.

Why Study?

Because studying is planned learning that can enrich your life, and can help you achieve whatever goals you have.

The more you know, the more you can do!

Do you have a specific goal which makes you want to study? Take time to think about this. What do you really want? How will studying help?

> *The most important thing about studying is your attitude and your desire to learn. Think positively.*

Studying is one of the biggest investments that you will make within yourself throughout your life. Don't let people negative actions become your reality. Reading is fundamental.

CHAPTER 4

How To Embrace Self- Esteem

Self-esteem is a measure of how much you appreciate yourself and recognize your own qualities, skills and achievements. It can also stem from how other people view you. A positive sense of self enables you to make healthy choices for your physical and mental well-being. It also gives you the courage to try new activities and socialize. A variety of free self-esteem activities can help you to overcome negative feelings.

Body image is a person's opinions, thoughts, and feelings about his or her own body and physical appearance. Having a positive body image means feeling pretty satisfied with the way you look, appreciating your body for its capabilities and accepting its imperfections.

Life Skills has a lot to do with your self concept. You must visualize yourself as beautiful, strong and in sound mind with the positive energy that you surround yourself with.

Promote high self esteem by practicing the following:

Self-care

Make a list of your positive qualities, skills and achievements. Laminate the list, hang it in your room and read it daily as a way to affirm yourself. Visualize the person described on that list. During those times when your confidence is shaken, create a VIP Kit. Fill a shoe box with photos of loved ones, cards, love letters, certificates of awards, report cards, job reviews and recommendations, inspirational poems and stories. Have family members write a handful of reasons why you're special and pop their notes into your VIP kit. Pull that kit out when you need to reaffirm your faith in yourself. Take time out of your schedule to nurture your spiritual side. Go to a park or take a hike and enjoy the natural world. Soak in a bath surrounded by lit candles. Crawl into bed and read a favorite book or listen to comforting music.

Exercise and Sports

Youngsters who engage in extracurricular physical activity tend to enjoy heightened levels of concentration and energy, elevated brain function, changes in musculature and increased self-esteem. As a result, they tend to do well academically. Regular exercise will help you to manage stress and improve your body image, both of which are connected to your self-esteem. Because exercise pumps up your endorphins, or neurotransmitters that produce the runner's high, it will help you to stay optimistic, focused and energetic. A brisk walk or jog daily, or simple weights that can be used at home, will provide you with enough exercise.

Hobbies and activities

Find a new hobby that will teach you a new skill, such as cooking, gardening and carpentry. If you have always wanted to learn a martial art, enroll in self-defense classes. Learn how to play a musical instrument if you're so inclined. Educate and challenge yourself in different ways to enhance your self-esteem. If you do not have the funds, join an online service where you can trade your skills. The Skills Exchange Service is a website where people barter their knowledge, such as paragliding, carpentry and computer programming.

Helping others

Volunteer your time to a nonprofit organization or charitable cause. By helping others, you help yourself. Not only is this activity free, but it can add considerable value to the lives of others. The appreciation that others will show you for generous acts will enhance your self-esteem. As well, such activities provide perspective. By interacting with people who are less privileged or disabled in any way, you may recognize the gifts that life has brought you

Your social circle affects your self-esteem

Self esteem is a state of mind and you have to moniturewho you let in. There will be a time in life when you have to let go of some of your fair whether friends and family and move on. Negative people cause stress, high blood pressure, heart disease and many other avoidable conditions. Here's the thing, all people are not malice but the handful that are deceitful can have such a negative impact on your life your head will spend. Learn to decipher who stays and who goes. Make a list of all the people that you can count on no matter what the circumstances. Then make a list of all the people who can sway either way. Last make a list of the Nay Sayers. After you have done that, put an X through the Nay Sayers and delete them from your phone. Then hold on to the Sayers because you may need them to do something for you. That's all they want you for so look at it as returning the favor. Last of all your dependable people will become your Ace in a Whole. Keep them around because as you grow they will help you stay focused and tell you the truth about yourself. We all need some truth serum once in a while. Now sit back and watch your life start revolving in a healthy direction

Develop a sound Mind, Body and Soul

Self esteem is developed mainly through external sources that are validated through physical appearance or being popular. Today we live in a world of judgment and misconception. You must create a personal foundation of self knowledge, love and confidence to survive. BEAUTY STARTS WITHIN so you must project a image of self acceptance and self image that makes you a winner. Feed your mind everyday with positive thoughts by saying to yourself, I look nice today or no matter what i face, God has my back. Get to know yourself, spend some time alone. Be honest and true to who you are. Stop thinking the next person has more than you. If you work long and hard enough your time will come. Learn to mind your own business and take responsibility for your choices and actions. Learn to accept yourself as you are and develop your abilities to be who you want to be not who you wish to be. Life is not fair and it sure is not easy to win but it is more rewarding in the end to go through the steps and stop trying to take short cuts.

When your self esteem and self concept are in tack, you will strut through life unbothered by the small things because the confidence you possess will present you as poised, assured and equipped to win in this game called life.

Chapter 5

Bullying

Bullying is never acceptable. Bullying is unwanted aggressive behavior toward a student or person that creates a power inbalance. This behavior is repeated over time. It includes actions such as making threats, starting rumors, attacking someone physically or verbally and excluding someone from a group on purpose. In this chapter we will discuss options on how to deal with this type of situation. Apart of learning LIFE SKILLS is knowing how to turn Life's negative energy into positive energy.

Why a bully might be targeting you

- ☐ **To look tough**
- ☐ **Because they are jealous of you**
- ☐ **To make themselves popular**
- ☐ **They're being bullied themselves**
- ☐ **To escape their own problems**

If you are being bullied, you are not alone. Thousands of people have this problem but that does not make it OK. Bullies are nothing more than scared, frightened people who are looking for acceptance and are afraid that they don't fit in so they have to bring attention to themselves by putting others down. All bullies are not bad people, they just need someone to love them and are often bullied themselves. Again, that does not excuse their bad behavior. Unless you have been bullied, you may not understand the devastation and anger it may cause in kids and young adults. Bullying can cause physical problems as well as make you feel frightened, depressed and sometimes suicidal. Often a bully will target you for no real reason except to make themselves look superior. Bullies may not like that you are different from the mainstream or may be new to the school. No matter how you slice it, They make you feel powerless, humiliated and alone. You may not want to go to school, class, practice, sports or even get on the bus. Whether the bulling is new or has been going on for a while, you must take the proper steps to put an end to it!! You deserve to be happy and treated with respect no matter what your race or gender, in fact you better demand it!!

Overcoming being bullied

There are positive steps you can take to stop and prevent bullying.

- ☐ **Tell an adult**- By telling your parent, guardian or teacher, the bully will deny it when confronted and back down because they don't want to look like a trouble maker in front of the adults that admire or think highly of them.
- ☐ **Walk away**- Since they want to feel superior over you and control your emotions, simply tell them in a, matter of fact way, that you are not interested in what they have to say and walk away. What you just did was take your power back and left them feeling puzzled.
- ☐ **Be confident**- just because you are different, quiet or like being by yourself doesn't mean that you are lacking confidence or don't deserve to exist and be happy. Tell the bully, in your confident voice, that you don't wish to engage in negative activities and that he/she need to go and find some positive things to do because you are busy. Keep your composure and leave.
- ☐ **Surround yourself with positive people or groups**-most of the time if you are with friends the bully will leave you alone because he/she knows that everybody is not afraid of him and he doesn't want you to have any allies.

Never let a bully control your life. Don't blame yourself, be proud of who you are and get help.

Gays and lesbians are particularly at risk of bullying. If you need help call

- ☐ In the U.S.: **1-866-4-U-TREVOR (488-7386)**
- ☐ In Canada: **1-877-OUT-IS-OK (688-1765)**
- ☐ In the UK: **0207 837 7324**
- ☐ In Australia: **1800 184 527**
- ☐ In New Zeal and: **(04) 473 7878**

There are different types of bullies

- ☐ **Physical Bullying-Hitting or pushing you**. This type of behavior should never be undermined as a display of love or kindness. Someone hitting you should always be seen as anger and you should tell an adult or someone close to you that will help.
- ☐ **Relationship bullying**- excluding someone from groups or activities, spreading lies or rumors about them, hazing, harassment or making someone do something they don't want to do. When you are in a relationship, don't give up your right to make good choices. You will succeed in life with or with out that person as long as you believe that you are beautiful, strong and smart.
- ☐ **cyber bullying**-Is when someone or people are bullying you on line, through email or text. They post bad information about you or pictures. Cyber bullying among young adults is unacceptable and wrong. its not OK to hurt people in any way

Either way BULLYING IS NOT EXCEPTABLE!!!!

Myths & Facts about bullying

Myth: My child would never be a bully

Fact: To all parents, kids make mistakes and because we are so quick to defend our kids, we deny them the help that is needed to make them responsible for their actions.

Myth: It's only bullying if someone is physically hurt.

Fact: Words hurt. If your child is constantly targeting another child with malice intentions to hurt their feelings, that's bullying.

Myth: Bullies are bad people and should be punished without knowing the situation

Fact: There are a lot of reasons why kids bully. Sometimes they are bullied and want someone else to feel there pain. Its not okay but its a temporary pain re leaver. Feeling stressed and overwhelmed are other reasons for bullies to act out.

Myth: Kids can only be bullies or victims

Fact: Not true. Kids can change roles. If they are bullied in middle school and then become popular in high school, they can now take on the bullying role to seek revenge.

Signs that your child may being bullied. It's worth looking in to

- ☐ Withdrawal from friends and activities
- ☐ Physical complaints
- ☐ Worried, moody or angry
- ☐ Nightmares
- ☐ Start to fail in school
- ☐ skips school
- ☐ missing items such as clothes, jewelry, electronics etc
- ☐ depressed or talks about not being good enough
- ☐ talks of suicide or running away
- ☐ weight fluctuation or loss of appetite
- ☐ comes home from school extra hungry or always have to use the bathroom like he/she couldn't use it all day

Parents, guardians and teachers must step in

Most of the time if your child is being bullied, they won't tell a parent or adult because they are embarrassed or they may think the bulling is temporary. It's your job as a parent to pay attention to your child and ask questions. The long term affect of bullying causes mental and physical damage. It will lower there self esteem and cause severe emotional harm.

As parents, guardians and teachers we must step in and let our children know that we love them and no mater what they are going through, we will help them.

Here are a couple of suggestions

- ☐ **Friends**-Try and talk to one of there close friends to see if your child has complained to them
- ☐ **School**-set up a meeting with their teachers, coaches and the principal to try and get some answers
- ☐ **Be relatable**-Tell them situations that may have happen to you or someone that you know when you where there age and how you handled it. Always have a clear mind when discussing this topic. Stay clear of being judgmental or confrontational with your child. They are already emotionally drained.
- ☐ **Empowerment**-Let them know that they are smart, talented and that nobody has the right to invade there space because they are different or don't want to be apart of the so called "IN CROWD". We are all unique in our own little way because God didn't make no junk.
- ☐ **Professional help**-This situation can be stressful to a parent as well, so if all fails take your child to a professional for help. Sometime bullying is hereditary. You may need counseling also

Signs that your child may be a bully;

- ☐ They always have extra money and they don't have a job
- ☐ They get into a lot of fights or display violent behavior toward their sibling or you
- ☐ They must win in everything and will go to any measures to do it
- ☐ They have new items that you didn't buy and they cant explain where they came from
- ☐ Does not take responsibility for there bad behavior
- ☐ Uses drugs or alcohol and hang around people that are bullies

How parents can help

It has been known that bulling can be a learned behavior just like being bullied. If you as a parent was a bully it may be displayed through abusing your children, spouse or friends. You may always talk negative or make fun of others because in your mind nobody is better than you or you may abuse workers at a restaurant, car wash or retail store implying that there job is worthless because they don't make top dollar like you do. Well i have news for you, those same people with hard work and dedication can work their way up to the top and be your boss one day or your children boss. Be careful what you put in the atmosphere, it might come back to bite you in the face one day.

The same goes for parents that have been bullied. Your lack of confidence and low self esteem shows up in your life and you are your children role model. Because you don't know how to cope with being a leader and standing up for yourself your child may take on those same traits. The apple don't fall far from the tree.

It doesn't matter which parent you where at this point, but what does matter is that you help your child to become the best adult possible leading by example. Talk to your kids about bullying and let them know that it is wrong. Tell them that there are consequences to pay in life for bad behaviour. Enforce rules and find out what is going on in your child day to day life. Being an active parent let's your child know that you care and will be there to guide them through this journey until they can navigate own their own

In life you will experience the good, bad and the ugly. You decide who you are and who you want to be. Bullying is never acceptable by you or to you

CHAPTER 6

HOW TO DEVELOP GOOD COMMUNICATION AND SOCIAL SKILLS

What is Communication?

Communication is simply the act of transferring information from one place to another using body language, gestures and the tone and pitch of your voice. Through out life you must communicate with others making communication another top priority in learning LIFE SKILLS. Developing good communication skills and learning how to transfer information properly will be important in your professional and personal life. You must learn to speak to a wide variety audience while maintaining good eye contact. Good communicators know how to tailor there speech to their audience.

Why good communication skills are necessary

Communication happens for a reason. Knowing how to speak or work in groups, listen effectively or write clearly and precisely are all necessary skills in the professional environment. Your employer will be looking to hire someone with those qualifications and more. Being a good communicator will improve your quality of life and help you to express your ideas to others. Listening is the number one communication skill. If you don't practice effective listening, messages are easily misunderstood causing a lot of unnecessary mistakes. Listening is so important in he work place that employers sometime have listening classes to help improve the quality of work produced, increase customer satisfaction and to create new and innovative ideas that will improve the company. Listening is positive energy that many entrepreneurs and leaders build there success upon. Good listening skills will be the foundation and building blocks to a successful career and life.

Why listening is so important in having good communication skills

Listening and hearing are not the same thing. Hearing is the sound that enters into your ears, its a physical process providing your hearing is OK. Effective listening involves more than just hearing someone speak, it requires focus and concentrated effort both mental and physical. Listening involves paying attention to not only what a person is saying but becoming involved in there story, in fact you must be just as invested in what the person is saying as they are. Pay attention to their verbal and non verbal communication, watch there body movements and facial expressions because your ability to listen effectively depends on how you perceive and understand these messages. Listening is one of the most powerful ways to connect with another person. You may sometime hear your parent say to you, "are you listening to me, not do you hear me, because listening and hearing are not the same thing." Sometime in life all someone wants you to do is JUST LISTEN.

Why non-verbal communication is so important

Non verbal communication conveys implicit messages whether intentional or not. Through non verbal expressions your body language speaks in volume. Non verbal signs such as facial expressions, your tone or pitch in your voice, body movements, eye contact or your behavior say more than words can express. People tend to have less control over there non verbal actions than the words coming out of their mouth which means when in doubt of what someone is really trying to say, go with the non verbal signs. A lack of non verbal signs may mean that the person is trying to control their body language and is hiding their true emotions.

Learning the language of non verbal communication is not easy but it is helpful when trying to reinforce what was just said in words, provide feed back to others and regulating the flow of a conversation. The bottom line is that non-verbal communication will always show you what a person is really thinking opposed to what they are saying. Actions speak louder than words.

How to develop effective communication skills

There are barriers that cause ineffective listening. For example when someone is speaking, instead of you listening to the entire story you are already planning your reply or defense. Sometimes you may be distracted by what someone else is saying in the room that you find more interesting or their appearance may cause you to lose focus. Whatever your reason, it still causes the same negative effect and may cause the speaker to either stop talking or become upset. The bottom line is always seek clarity in what a speaker is saying by using your Effective listening Skills so that you can be productive in your school surrounding, work environment and personal life.

The break down

- ☐ **Learn to listen** -without being judgmental toward other people thoughts
- ☐ **Encourage others**- it is not all about you, congratulate others on their accomplishments as well. Team work makes the dream work
- ☐ **Treat people equally**- avoid patronizing and talking behind peoples back. By treating people equal to each other and showing empathy, you will build trust and respect.
- ☐ **Understand why communication fails**--when communicating stay calm and focused, gather your information first and then have room for negotiation. These ideas almost always work in maintaining good relationships in life
- ☐ **Use your interpersonal communication skills-**interpersonal skills are life skills that we use everyday when interacting with people in person. These are subconscious actions that we take for granted. You are using your interpersonal skills when you walk in a room, engage

in conversations, make decisions, solve problems and work in goups. It's just another name for communication skills broken down into everyday life work. Without good interpersonal skills it will be hard to master other life kills and be a successful healthy adult because they are used everyday and in all aspect of your life.

What are social skills?

Social skills are the skills we us to communicate or interact with each other verbally and non- verbally through gesture, body language and our personal appearance. We are all sociable creatures. Developing social skills is about how we communicate with each other. Social skills, listening, verbal & non verbal communication are all important skills to understand if you want to be a successful adult. Getting along with and understanding people will be the key to opening up many doors that can lead to life long friendships or careers.

Here are some advantages of having good social skills:

- ☐ **Being a leader**-Social skills can be taught, practiced and learned. In life you can be a leader or follower, it's your choice. If you are surrounded by strong, goal setting adults who are outgoing and have positive ideas you may learn to be charismatic which is an important trait of a successful leader. Charismatic people use there skill to get people on their side or to see their point of view which is a great communication skill in the work place, especially if you are going for a management or supervisor position.
- ☐ **Better friendships**- Having good social skills will help you choose better friends because you will learn what type of people you like and will spend your time with like minded people. Positive friendship will help boost your self esteem and reduce stress.
- ☐ **Advance your career**- Having good social skills will help you work better in a team and teach you how to influence others to get things done. A good team leader under stands different personalities and knows how to motivate and influence people to get things done. All companies look for people that can generate sales and make the work environment pleasant.

What is Character Development?

Character development is the process of learning attitudes, beliefs and behaviors that are important for people to have as responsible citizens. Good character sets ground rules in life for young adults and adults to learn and practice behaviors that reflect ethical values. Due to the lack of character development their is a high pregnancy rate, drunk driving, violence and substance abuse among teens and young adults. Clearly adults need to do a better job of teaching high standards of behavior and self value in the family, communities and schools. Young adults need a consistent message of responsibility, respect, caring, trustworthiness, justice and leadership which all fall under the character development umbrella. Character development is a long term life skill that will produce mentally healthier adults that will respect consequences. Developing a high standard of self respect and disciple will create a winning team of productive young adults with a life time of positive energy to pass on. When you know better, you do better.

Good communication and social skills, lead to good leadership skills which is an essential part of life. Social skills and character development are harder to attain as you get older so the sooner you start, the better.

CHAPTER 7

JOB VS CAREER

There's nothing wrong with being content with doing a job. However, every job you take is crucial to the development of your career. You will spend a lifetime in whatever job or career choice you make so take your time to decide who you want to be when you grow up. Choosing a career will change the path of your life so do a self evaluation assessment, dream big and map out a plan that you can navigate through for years to come.

Here are some tips on choosing a job vs career

- ☐ A job will give you financial security to reach your goals, a career will pay you for your talents and skills throughout your life.
- ☐ Getting a job does not involve any planning, a career consist of schooling, evaluating your work style and planning
- ☐ A job is work that you do to get paid, a career is a path that you take that pays you to do a hobby or skill that you love.
- ☐ A job is low risk with little flexibility and stability, a career is exciting, high risk and unpredictable while taking calculated risk
- ☐ A job will fit your lifestyle, a career will bring out your personal aspirations and align with your talents
- ☐ A job becomes less satisfying over time because you are not taping into your creative side, a career is a roller coaster ride that allows you to use your passion, interests and gifts that you where born with

- ☐ A job you work to live, a career you live to work

Advice for Teens Preparing to Choose a Career

Think about what you enjoy, and then find out how you can get paid to do it.

Your teen years are the ideal time for you to explore many different options before deciding on the best one for you. It can take a long time to decide on a career path, and you might change your mind at any step along the way. Do not feel obligated to follow through on an initial choice even when you find that you are no longer as interested in it as you once were. Many people end up in the right careers for them accidentally or by simply doing what they love and getting paid for it.

Use Your Parents or Guardians for Help

☐ Your parents or guardians can be of tremendous help to you because they know you well and can suggest possible careers based on your personality, interests and strengths. Ask them for advice, but make sure they are not imposing their wishes on you. Parents and guardians can also help by showing you some aspect of their careers over the years. Do you want to emulate them, or do you want to do something completely different? Think about the reasons for your answer, and explore career paths that support those reasons.

See a Career Counselor at School

☐ Career counselors help advise people on the right paths to take for their immediate future goals and beyond. You can make an appointment with them and have a discussion about your concerns over choosing the right career. They can be of help whether you are completely undecided as to what to do or whether you already have several options you are considering. They also have personality tests they can give you to help reveal your strengths and the best possible careers for you.

CHOOSE a Career Based on Your Strengths

☐ We all want to do something that we are good at. What better way to find out what you are good at than to see what subjects you constantly perform well in and enjoy in school. Although not all careers are directly subject related, adopting this strategy can give you some ideas. Otherwise, you might think of some other activities that you enjoy such as public speaking, fashion design or sales, and find out careers that depend primarily on those skills.

Choose a Career Based on Your Future Aspirations

☐ Some people aspire to have time to spend with their families and therefore rule out careers that involve a lot of travel, such as those with the aviation industry and high-profile medical careers. Others want to ensure that they are secure financially; therefore, they seek out careers that offer higher compensation when compared to others. You should think about what kind of life would make you happiest and try to find a career to fit that goal.

Research

☐ Find out as much as you can about different careers before you decide on one. You can conduct research on the Internet, in a public library or at your school. Make sure the information you find is up-to-date. Find out what kind of education you need, how you will fund your education and how many years it might take you to get established in that field. These questions can help you narrow your choices as you decide on the best career for you.

Parents

Helping Your 11th or 12th Grader with Career Preparation and "Fit"

As the parent of an eleventh or twelfth grader), how confident are you about your teen's plans for the future? Does your teen have realistic job or career goals? Has your teen found enjoyable activities that he is enthusiastic about pursuing as an adult? Has your teen held volunteer or paid part-time jobs? If so, can he see any of his jobs leading to a career that will allow him to be an independent, working adult?

Now that your teen is in the last two years of high school, what kinds of help and support can you provide as he or she prepares for the future? First, ask yourself what "success" for your teen means to you. Does it mean the same thing to your teen? Now's the time to redefine success based on your teen's unique strengths and interests. Keep in mind that success involves good health and strong relationships, as well as satisfying work.

Career Development

Whatever your teen's path to the world of work is Career management is an important life skill to learn. Whether they choose post secondary education or training, or directly to a job -- it can be helpful to consider the stages of career development. Statistics say that a person will change careers (not jobs) 5-7 times in a lifetime.

Steps to career development

- ☐ **interest assessment**- in this stage you will find out your values, strengths and weakness and a sense of self awareness and who you are. This is where your life work begins.
- ☐ **Work style investigation**-This stage is characterized as the stage of confusion. There are so many opportunities in the work force that finding a perfect fit for you can be a bit overwhelming. Remember to stay focused and keep a positive mind set and investigate your options.
- ☐ **Preparation phase**-In this stage you are excited to get started on your lifes work. You must now set goals and stay positive because you have a lot of work ahead of you. Do research to gain more knowledge and experience.
- ☐ **Job or career**-In this phase you have committed to a career of your choose and feel that this is what you where meant to do. You may have known all along but now have finally committed to it. Stay focused and keep your eye on the prize.

☐ **Commitment stage**- in this phase you feel comfortable in your career. Start building a business network and continue to stay current with industry standards

☐ **transition stage**- in this phase you will feel the need to either advance to another level or change careers altogether. You will get a feeling of discomfort because you don't know what you will be doing next. Now will be the time to make conscious changes in your career decision. You will start from interest assessment and reevaluate your life work.

Life after high school

Your prayers have been answered, You have prayed to be an adult all your childhood life. You want to make your own decisions, stay out late and be responsible for your own well being, well here is your chance but you have to be prepared. You can walk through the revolving door from childhood to adulthood and finally show the world who you are. No amount of preparation will guarantee success but here are a few pointers that may be helpful in your transition, even though you should start these preparations your senior year in high school.

☐ **Life skills**-learning how to cook and do laundry are necessary life skills and will be discussed in future chapters

☐ **time management and goal setting**- learning to use your time wisely and setting realistic goals are important to being a responsible adult. Read the first chapters for more details.

☐ **buy an alarm clock**- you must master being on time to work or school. Your parents should not be responsible for getting your day started

☐ **learn to backup data**-learning how to back up data is an essential skill in life since most of your work will be done on a computer.

☐ **Drinking and drugs**-If you must drink, do it responsibly. Have a designated driver and never leave a drink unattended because someone may slip something in it that may cause you temporary or permanent damage. Be honest with yourself about the pros and cons of drugs and alcohol.

- ☐ **appointments and phone calls**- learn to make necessary calls like making doctor and dentist appointments. This will teach you how to advocate for yourself and plan ahead.
- ☐ **Money**- learn how to open up a bank account and learn to master the art of paying yourself first. Make sure you discuss with your parents if you should apply for a credit card now and how to use it responsibly. These life skills are discussed in later chapters
- ☐ **stay focused**--last but not least stay focused. You are now considered an adult and if you break the law you will be charged as an adult. Choose your friends and your situations wisely.

You will jump over many hurtles, some big and some small in your new pursuit to find your divine purpose. It will be a lot easier if you have set goals and exit plans to assist you along the way.

Your journey will now begin

Choosing a college

Summer orientation is vey important when entering into your freshmen year. If it is offered, i recommend that you take it. Even though you have probably visited the college several times throughout your senior year in high school becoming an official student will present different expectations.

Reasons to attend summer orientation:

- ☐ **Get to know the college**-This will give you a head start on getting to know where thing are on the campus as well as eating in the dining area and sleeping in the dorms.
- ☐ **Get to meet other students**-It will be very exciting to meet other students with the same interest and backrounds. Sometimes close alliances are formed and roommates are even chosen. Often these grow into close friendships and you can start your freshmen year with a circle of friends waiting.
- ☐ **Get to meet the administration-Getting** to know who your go to people are and what to expect from the school will release some of he stress of being in unfamiliar territory away from home.

☐ **Adjust to your new college life**-There will be a lot of informative information given out at orientation that can better equip you for your transition from a high school senior to a college freshmen. If you can, take advantage of this opportunity because it will definitely give you a jump on things.

So you have been chosen to go to 5 different colleges, How do you select the right one? Here are some suggestions:

☐ **Revisit your short list**-In the beginning of your college process determine why you chose those colleges and decide why they may be a good fit for you

☐ **Look for priorities**-Where is it located, can you stay on campus or do they have sports or clubs that you may want o join

☐ **Revisit your top 3 schools**-Way out the pros and cons. Take a list of questions that will help you to make a good choice

☐ **Which school fits your major**-Check out the college rankings but remember academic prestige can be measured on a smaller scale as well. Which school is better known for your major and is the faculty invested in helping you succeed

☐ **Which school will offer you grants or scholarships-Compare** aid awards, which school offers more financial aid and grants(free money) and loans(money you pay back).

☐ **Which school is better for your end game**-Your purpose for attending college is to pinpoint a great job or career, decide which school will help you reach those goals.

☐ **Job placement**-which college has the highest rate of helping with career placement. Investigate each schools career centers and ask questions about job fairs

☐ **Move on from rejection**- don't focus on the schools that didn't except you, focus on the opportunities ahead

☐ **Don't procrastinate**- you may be tempted to want to stay out a year and work to save up some money, but don't do it. If you can start immediately after high school, keep your education flowing while you can.

Maybe college is not for you, there are other options like trade schools and military careers. I went to a college and attended a trade school afterwards. You may find your life work by pursuing a career that require hands on skills like a cosmetologist, Acting, comedian, photography, modeling, contractor, mechanic, hvac worker etc. Don't let other people talk you out of your dreams by telling you that these are not real careers. I choose cosmetology and my life seems to be working out just fine.

Here are some benefits of going to a Trade school:

- ☐ **A trade is something that nobody can take from you**- the skill that you are blessed to have goes with you everywhere in life. You can use it at anytime and anywhere
- ☐ **Less time to train**- most trade schools are 2 years or less. You can now get a job directly in your career field and not have to look around or take unwanted jobs until an opportunity presents itself in your carer choice. The highest benefit to me is that if you are looking to be an Entrepreneur having a trade is definitely the way to go.
- ☐ **Expenses**- The average cost of attending a trade school is about $10,000 a year, which creates far less student loan debts to pay back.

Here are some tips to help choose a vocational/Trade school:

- ☐ **School size**-make sure that the school has shared academic and hands on training available because the book knowledge is just as important as the training.
- ☐ **Hands on training**-the hands on training is critical when choosing a vocational school. There is no better way to learn than to actually do it yourself. Check to see if the field you are interested in has the proper equipment to train you.
- ☐ **Retention rate**-How many students graduate from there schools and actually pursue a career in the field that they studied. High drop out rates could mean that the schools program didn't meet there expectations

☐ **Accreditation status**-An accredited school is the key to your financial aid. Not only that but your degree will be taken serious. Your goal is to ensure your future success

☐ **Modern equipment**-- make sure the equipment is modern. Your goal is to graduate and start in the work force immediately and well prepared. You must learn on up to date equipment in order to achieve that goal.

Choosing a military career

Enlisting in the military can be exciting and beneficial. Who is in charge? The President of the U.S. is the Commander in Chief(who is responsible for all final decisions), the Secretary of The Department of Defense(DOD) has control of the military and each branch except the Coast Guard which is under the Department of Homeland Security. This career choice is great for anyone who like or need discipline and structure in there life.

The U.S. Armed Forces are made up of five armed service branches: Air Force, Army, Coast Guard, Marine Corp, Navy. Each branch has its own mission.

There are three categories;

☐ **Active Duty**-full time soldier and sailors
☐ **Reserve and Guard Forces** -usually work a civilian job but can be called to full time active duty
☐ **Veterans & Retirees-past member of the military**

What are the benefits of joining the military?

The military offer many incentives for joining there branches. Here are a few tips

Student loan programs- If you are going to college or want to attend college, the military may have programs to assist you in repayment of the loans

Voluntary Educational Programs- Each branch of he service has their own educational program that will help you reach your educational goals. They may include tuition assistance, classroom counseling and other systems to support your educational needs.

G.I Bill- The G.I Bill is designed to help service members and eligible veterans cover the cost of getting an education or training. There are several programs depending on the person eligibility and status. The benefits covers Active Duty members, Selective Reserves and National Guard Armed Forces and their families.

Special Forced Recruitment- The Army, Navy and Air Force offer special incentives for those signing up for Special Force Programs. You should only chose these programs if you are in great physical and mental shape because they are extremely competitive.

Guaranteed pay check;free room and board- You won't get rich but you will receive a guaranteed pay check on the first and fifteenth

Paid vacations-You earn 25 days of leave every month which translates into 30 days of paid vacation time per year

military discounts;free flights- All you have to do is find the nearest MAC flight (military flight) and sign up. There is a chance you may get bumped so always have a plan B

Free health care- Doctor visits, dentist visits or even get into an accident; as long as you survive the military has got you covered for FREE.

Training -Everybody gets a good amount of training that will help them in some way when thy get out. Military training on your resume doesn't look bad either.

Travel-Depending on the branch, you have the change to be stationed all over the world. An opportunity you may not have had if you didn't join the service

The world is yours. There are Pros and Cons to choosing all careers. Make sure you do your research before choosing a career for you. Everything is not for everybody

FINANCIAL AID AND GRANT GUIDES

FinAid!
Provides a comprehensive source of student financial aid information, advice and tools.
www.finaid.org/

Free Application for Federal Student Aid (FAFSA)
Supports post secondary education by providing money for college to eligible students and families.
www.fafsa.ed.gov/

FastWeb
Provides information on scholarships, internships, and jobs.
www.fastweb.com/

Grants.gov
Provides access to annual federal and state awards on over 1,000 grant programs.
www.grants.gov/

National Association of Student Financial Aid Administrators (NASFAA)
Provides sources of financial aid to students.
www.nasfaa.org/Redesign/ParentsStudents.html

ScholarshipsAndGrants.us
Discover financial aid, scholarships and grants no matter what your major.
http://www.scholarshipsandgrants.us/

Cappex
Offers free assistance to help students find their ideal college fit and the scholarships to pay for it.
http://www.cappex.com

College Board
Provides information about college costs, scholarships, financial aid applications, education loans, and college financing.
www.collegeboard.com/student/pay/index.html

EdFund
Provides student loan services under the Federal Family Education Loan Program.
www.edfund.org/wps/portal/

What ever career path you take, remember what God has for YOU is for YOU!! Don't let negative people influence your life. Surround yourself with winners and game changers. Be careful who you ask for advice. Accomplishing something is the easier part, maintaining and keeping it is when the real work and dedication kicks in.

CHAPTER 8

SEEK AND MAINTAIN EMPLOYMENT

CAREER ADVICE FROM ME:

I've spent every day falling more madly in love with how I live my life and spend my time, the contributions I'm making to society, and the discomfort and growth that I feel each day.

My journey getting here was both exhausting and frustrating. It was not at all straightforward. I had numerous experiences that collectively brought me here, teaching me what I'm capable of and showing me what does and does not resonate.

Though I've known for many years that my purpose was to teach, it took me some time to fully embrace my intuition, to figure out how to actualize this vision, and to build the courage to lean into my fears. (And it's still, and always will be, an ongoing learning process.)

How do you know that you are on your career path?

- ☐ **You picked something that you are good at-** When you have picked a job that you are good at and can get paid to do it, you have found your lifes work. Ask yourself, "Is this a job that i would do for free"? If the answer is "yes" then you are passionate about your choice and passion will get you through hard times.
- ☐ **Your job doesn't seem like work-**When it is time to go home and you have given it your all and cant wait to do it all again tomorrow

or your work seems like a lifestyle instead of your job, you are in your career. You will be constantly pursuing your vision of who you want to be and it will be aligned with who you are.

- ☐ **You are willing to suffer-**There will be road blocks, speed bumps and set backs but you are willing to take on the short term pain as a challenge to learn and grow because you know that the reward of winning will a beautiful sight. A set back is a set up for a stronger come back.

- ☐ **You enjoy life-**You live in integrity because your lifes work is an extension of who you are. You can enjoy life when you have time for fitness, family and fun yet your instinct and desire to work keeps you motivated and goal orientated through out the day.

- ☐ **You are committed-**You have no doubt in your mind that this work is for you. Your heart says "yes". People that matter notice your excitement and dedication and will want to encourage you. At first people that are close to you may discourage you because they don't want to see you fail but eventually they will come around when they see that you will stop at nothing to be successful.

How to rock your next job interview

- ☐ The main key is mental preparation which can mean the difference between victory(getting the job) and defeat (looking in the classifieds). Visualize in your mind how the interview will go. Here are a few pointers:
- ☐ Write down all of your strengths and the skills you used to achieve them and how you can make a difference in the company
- ☐ Write down all your weaknesses and how you will improve them by signing up for training classes and attending seminars
- ☐ You can take on line job interview test. This will help prepare you and relieve some of your anxiety
- ☐ Do some research on the company that you are interviewing with. This will help you with dialogue when you are asked certain questions like, Why do you think this company is a good fit for you?

☐ Don't Brown nose- giving a compliment is okay but never over compliment the interviewer and be careful how you say it. You don't want o seem disingenuous.

☐ Be available during interview hours- Interview hours are usually between 8am-5:30pm. Asking an interviewer to do a phone interview after hours can sometime be seen a disrespectful.

☐ Be on time- Arriving to early or to late is not good. A good time to arrive is 15 mins early even if you have to get there and wait in your car until that time. Fifteen minutes will give you time to gather your thoughts and calm down.

What to consider before taking a job offer

☐ **Leverage**- Find out what the fair market salary is for the job. Never give an exact amount of how much you want to get paid, only a ball park figure. This will leave room for them to make the first move and you can act off of your leverage.

☐ **Look at the big picture**- How does this job fit into your career path. This will help you to advocate for yourself better because you know that this can be a stepping stone to your big picture.

☐ **Consider the benefits**-Take into consideration if the hours and schedule works for you and let the interviewer know that you will be on time and your hours are flexible if need be. Also check into their health care plan, vacation and sick days.

☐ **Culture**-Does the work environment agree with your work ethics. For example, you don't like quiet closed in places you wouldn't work at a library. If you like to travel maybe you would seek a job as a flight attendant.

10 Tips for Getting Hired

1. Would I hire ME?

Get a deeper understanding of what hiring managers are looking for, which will help you improve your interviewing skills and market yourself better as a potential employee. Don't go for a manager's position wearing a sweat suit, although that's appropriate to get a job as a personal trainer at a gym.

2. Don't be afraid to follow up.

Job seekers sometimes worry that following up will be perceived as too aggressive, but that's rarely the case. Companies want to work with employees who are excited about working in the organization, and checking in after an interview, either via e-mail or with a thank-you note, demonstrates initiative.

3. Use the internet to keep track of job openings.

Make job boards work for you by subscribing to new posts using a Google Reader. Run your search query by location and industry, and pull those specialized results into your feed. That will allow you to quickly and easily look through new job openings and star ones that interest you.

4. Seek out non-profit organizations.

Expand your network and skills through volunteering. Nonprofit organizations are hungry for helpers who don't mind getting their hands dirty, and volunteering is an opportunity to gain valuable skills for your future career. It's also a great way to expand your network; you might meet a new industry contact or someone who's willing to serve as a reference.

5. Use Linked In to learn about your target companies.

Before sending your resume, check out Linked In's Companies feature. Look at New Hires to see who just landed a job, and ask those employees how to target your approach. You may also learn about job opportunities that aren't yet advertised by talking with former employees listed in Departures.

6. Create a digital-friendly resume.

Tweak your resume so it's easily up loadable, down loadable, and scan able. That means no bullets, boxes, boldface, unusual fonts, or indenting. Make it rich in keywords that will speak to employers in your field, terms that will stick out not only for a computerized search, but also for the in-person resume reader.

7. Consider taking a step back to keep moving forward.

If you can't get the job you want in 2014, stop whining and take anything you can get. Then keep right on looking. You don't owe an employer anything more than a day's work for a day's pay, so act in your own self-interest. You may even be more appealing to your dream employer if you're working.

8. Network with like-minded people.

Networking without a purpose is called socializing—and that's unlikely to deliver strong job leads or new contacts with target companies. Instead, go to events attended by people you want to connect with, share specific job-search objectives, and look to make targeted, strategic connections.

9. Use Social Media to help

Do your homework before tailoring your resume. To attract the attention of a hiring manager, you'll want to tailor your resume for each specific company. To do this well, you have to know the company well. So do your homework: review their website, read company reviews on Glassdoor.com, and follow the company on Twitter, Linked In, and Facebook.

10. Become a mentor

Look for opportunities to mentor a student or young colleague. If you put the effort in, mentoring can be about more than giving back. The experience may help you uncover new perspectives and ideas about your own career goals and how to achieve them. And it can be a resume-builder, too

SPECIAL REPORT: CLASSIC ETIQUETTE SITUATIONS IN BUSINESS AND HOW TO HANDLE THEM.

Your training program includes specific instructions for you and your clients about handling the most common etiquette mistakes and about applying etiquette to common business situations: Such as;

☐ **Networking and meeting new people -Always be professional when meeting new people related to business and try not to get into any personal conversations that may seem awkward.**

- ☐ running effective meetings-Use your time wisely and stick to the topic. Try to get feedback from your co -workers. This will keep them enthusiastic and involved in the companies success
- ☐ preventing distracting behaviors in the office-Dress for success at your work place so that people take you serious
- ☐ managing conflict -Never take matters into your own hands if you have a disagreement at work. Ask to speak with management or the boss so their is someone available to mediate
- ☐ setting boundaries- Always give and receive respect. Treat people how you want to be treated. Try to refrain from profanity
- ☐ ordering meals and dining at restaurants during business meetings- Use your inside voice. Have a great time but stay focused on what the meeting is based on.
- ☐ Respect other people time- Arrive early so that you don't keep your clients waiting. Not using time management can make or break a business deal

DRESS FOR SUCCESS

Common questions and answers

Q: What color suit should be worn for job interview?
A: black, navy blue or gray

Q: What color tie should one wear to a job interview?
A: One thing you can try if you have time before the interview date is to go to the place of business and look at the people as they come to or leave work and see how they are dressed.

Q: What is the best nail polish color for a job interview?
A: Nothing too bright and flashy, something simple. A French manicure, nothing to bold..

Q: What is the best color to wear on a job interview?

A: For men and women, always wear a suit. Colors should be low-key unless you are applying in the entertainment industry

Makeup and Clothes for Job Interviews

If you are applying for a job in an office environment that is considered conservative. Employment interviewers are often strongly affected by a job applicant's appearance, the right color choice and cosmetics do increase the chance of getting hired.

Here are some tips for conservative jobs:

Clothes- Think preppie, not sexy. Wear dark gray, navy blues or black. Keep it simple and classy

Accessories- Tone down the accessories. Wear cream, white or ivory, these colors show security. Silver jewelry is less flashy and coordinates well with basic colors. Black or dark color shoes with a matching pocketbook will keep your fashion statement up to par.

Hair- Nothing to fancy, a simple pulled back bun or a blow dry and curl will do fine. If you are wearing braids or twist, make sure that they are neat and clean.

Skip steel gray or green clothes; these storm associated colors make some interviewers anxious. Never wear all gray either, add a blouse or shirt with color to the ensemble to avoid looking drab or boring.

Creative jobs or Entertainment field

Clothes- The creative job fields like graphic design, cosmetology and fashion or makeup artistry are not so strict; yellow, bright blue, hot pink or purple may be worn with impunity. Jet black with touches of strong contrasting color emanates a vibe of mental stimulation. Orange accessories with a black outfit are perceived as cheerful, but don't go overboard. (Think happy, not Halloween). Wearing some jeans with a blazer will also accent your style

Accessories- Costume jewelry will stand out, remember in this industry more is OK. You would want to be trendy. Stylish shoes and bag to match. Name brands are also accepted especially if you are interviewing for their brand.

Hair- your hair should be sharp and well kept. A nice short or long cut or even ponytail styles will go over well. If you are wearing a weave or lace front wig, make sure it is freshly done and looks natural. There is nothing like a nice hairstyle or fresh male haircut to set off your outfit.

Makeup Colors and Makeup Application for Job Interviews

Conservative job

Conservative job interviewers respond very poorly to bright red or dark vampire lipstick, nail polish or blush colors. Glitter or iridescence anywhere on the face or body is a big no-no for traditional office applicants.

Make sure all face makeup is in the same general color family, natural or pinks always work. Never match the eye shadow with your shirt, shoes or pocketbook for this look is straight out of the 50's. It gives off an unsophisticated and unreliable employee image.

Creative jobs or Entertainment field

The face is just as influential as the clothes an interviewer wears. Brighter more flamboyant eye shadows, lipsticks (red, orange) and blushes are all only appropriate when applying for a creative position. Even in these cases, you must be careful not to come across as nutty. If you wear purple eye shadow tone it down by wearing a Smokey eye or muted shades in the crease and all over the lid.

TIP-Don't apply makeup to thick, blend carefully and check your makeup right before the interview. Mascara clumps, smeared shadow and lipstick in the teeth can be a deal breaker. If your clothes, makeup and hair are well thought out; there is nothing left to say but YOU'RE HIRED, HOW SOON CAN YOU START.

BEAUTY TIPS

1. When using an eye shadow primer, only place the primer where you'll be adding color.

2. "Cream rouge [blush] should be the first thing that touches your cheeks when you want to project an image of healthy and pinched cheeks

3. If you choose to use false eyelashes, remember to use the dark glue as it will blend in with the lashes.

4. Use a facial exfoliate bi-weekly to get dead skin off. Makeup will look better on a clean, smooth canvas.

5. After using a hair conditioning mask, follow with "a cold water rinse to close the hair cuticles

6. To get your braid to last all day, try styling hair that's "dirty with product". This will make the style stick longer.

7. If you have chipped nail-polish, add crackle or glitter on top to disguise the look of chipping.
8. Use a pumice stone on your feet after the shower to get rid of calluses on your feet.
9. Hydrate your under-eye area with an eye cream to prevent puffiness and bags.
10. If you often find yourself being too tired to wash your face at night, keep makeup removing wipes in your night stand to prevent a runny mess or morning break out.
11. The best way to get rid of ingrown hairs is to exfoliate, "which rids the skin of dead cells and allows the hair to break through the surface"
12. The best time to apply creams is after the shower, as the skin has been DE-oiled.
13. Replace mascara and liquid eyeliner after three to four months.
14. To keep hair color vibrant longer, use shampoos and conditioners formulated for colored hair.
15. Use a cream or milk cleanser to wash your face. Creams are less drying than gels.

GO TO MoniqueDonyaleCollection.com FOR ALL YOUR BEAUTY NEEDS!!!!

We sell skin care, make up, 100% virgin human hair bundles, hair care products & boutique.

Also visit MoniqueDonyaleDominicanSalon.com for all your hair service needs

Beauty starts within!!!!

CHAPTER 9

MONEY MATTERS

I was shocked. People were lost in the game of money with no road map of what to do or how to win the game. I couldn't punch this in my navigation or Map Quest to find my way this time. When I reached my late -20's, I realized that I knew very little about managing my money even though i had opened up a business by then. I knew how to save but i didn't know how to make my money work for me and if i was going to learn i would have to teach myself.

What does financial responsibility mean?

Teaching your young adult or yourself that money matters and how to make it work for you is a very important life skill. Here are some tips:

- **Pay yourself first**-Spending all your money on bills and putting money in everybody else pocket first will leave you with no savings for a rainy day. Always put money aside first (which is paying yourself) to invest in your future

- **Learn the value of waiting** -financial freedom is your choice. Learn to buy what you need, not what you want when you are goal oriented. Staying focused will definitely pay off in your future

- **How your credit factors in**--Student loans is the number one reason why a lot of people credit score is low. You will need your credit to establish assets and equity in life. Pay attention to your credit and get your free report once a year

- **Beware of the small spending**- Save early, save often. Eating out a lot is a good example of small spending. Try putting the money you would have spent on lunch for one week in an envelope and take your lunch instead. Watch how much money you would have saved.

- **Know the state of your money**- budgeting is very important to keeping track of your spending.

- **Your level of freedom is tied closely to your level of debt**-Make money grow by putting it o work for you. The more debt you accumulate the less freedom you will have to move around the world

BUDGETING

Try out Mint.com or Wesabe.com. These sites will help you and your grad create a budget in no time.

Many teens and young adults come out of high school and college without any experience in money management. Typically, they've been pulled into a sense of permanent financial security by family support. In the past, when bills needed to be paid their parents were always there to make them go away.

It is essential to teach young adults financial management early and to also put it in practice in your own life so teens will learn by example. I started out teaching the values of saving and careful money management early with my daughter who is now 20.

Good budgeting consists of learning the value of money and how to set a budget

The Value of Money

This discipline should be taught early and often. The best way to teach the value of money is to insist that they earn it. When children are as young as five or six, parents can consider not offering automatic allowances. Instead, set a pay scale for such tasks as bed making, dish washing, laundry gathering, pet care and other chores. This teaches the value that work equals money. When the children are older, they should be encouraged to earn money working outside the home. The jobs could include babysitting, lawn mowing, doing someone's hair, newspaper delivery etc.

Using eBay is also a great way for young entrepreneurs to learn responsibility, money values and money management. A good house cleaning can turn up many potential eBay items or the family can create crafts or buy items at wholesale prices to sell.

Set a Budget

When the young adults are in high school and college, parents should advise them on methods of controlling their money. The young adults will learn by day-to-day experience how spending should not exceed money coming in. By independently managing their own checkbook accounts, they'll know at all times how much money they have available for spending. Parents can also involve young adults in family budget planning. While doing research for this book, I stumbled upon a game called "The Money Game. If you can fit it in your budget, it's a good game to purchase.

Being a CEO myself at 26, I learned these principals, I called them the ;

FAKE IT UNTIL YOU MAKE IT GUIDELINES

1. **Save more than you spend**. If you want to live your life by choice and not by design you can't always wear designer clothes. You must choose to be thirty with a twist, always buy what you need not what you want or you will never be financially free to let your money work for you.

2. **Pay yourself first**. This does not mean when you receive your check you take out $300 and go to the mall and buy some stilettos or some new sneakers. What it means is to take a percentage of your earnings and put it into an investment that will make money for you while you sleep. This habit will eventually allow you to be your own boss or at least financially secure

3. **Dedication and goal setting**. Through dedication and goal setting your life will never be at a standstill. You will be allowing yourself the flexibility to seek higher financial success; which can be devastating if you are not navigating through life following goals.

4. **Never be the smartest person in your group**. If you want to learn how to be financially free then you must allow yourself to be vulnerable. Always be around people that you can learn from. By allowing yourself this privilege you will open the door to what we call FAVOR.

5. **Create 5 checks**. Never put all of your eggs in one basket. Find out what you want to specialize in, then create other outlets that can make you money stemming from that plan of action. For example, I have a production company called Monique Donyale Productions which is called my DBA or(Doing Business As). I also have other companies under the company's name (called Alternative Names) such as Monique Donyale skin care system, Make-Up & hair extension collection, Monique Donyale hair care system etc. I'm sure you get the message. Go to MoniqueDonyaleProductions.com

6. **Budgeting**. You must always budget in order to stay in your spending scope. Creating a budget or an itemized list of your

monthly financial obligations, due dates and amount owed will allow you to Pay Yourself first and your bills.

I'm sure you will hear these principals said to you throughout your life in many different ways but what you choose to do with them will determine your destiny.

checking & saving accounts

SAVING STRATEGIES

Saving and investing early

A few hundred dollars a month, invested regularly and carefully by a young adult, along with compound interest, can grow to a million dollar retirement savings account. When young adults are earning regular income, parents should advise them on the benefits of long-term money growth. They should be encouraged to begin intelligent investments, payroll savings and other regular plans for future financial security.

When young adults become older, their parents should continue to be there for them when loving advice and encouragement are needed.

It is essential that parents take the lead on teaching money skills by setting an example of good behavior … and by coaching good money behavior.

"Well before you give them a card, you have to have already taught them how the banking and payment system works in Canada; what an account is; how ins and outs — debits and credits -- affect your account; how to get more money in … how balances will change and what impacts that; what interest is and how you earn it; services fees and more."

Whether they're earning an income or hitting up the bank of Mom and Dad, making that cash last is an valuable skill. There are lots of ways parents can get their children more interested in family finances.

It starts with teaching them the system and then giving them increasingly more control over the system as they can handle it, Adding a hands-on approach is the most effective.

"Everything from taking their kids to the bank with them, explaining how to write a cheque and what it is, providing debit cards, teaching how getting a part time job can fill up one's bank account, explaining the value of money and how much something is worth, what it means to run out of money, talking about business news in the world and how it can affect interest rates … and much more.

Savings and checking accounts

Savings account meaning- account are accounts maintained by retail Financial institutions that pay interest but cannot be used directly as money in the narrow sense of a medium of exchange (for example, by writing a cheque). These accounts let customers set aside a portion of their liquid assets while earning a monetary return. For the bank, money in a savings account may not be callable immediately and in some jurisdictions, does not incur a reserve requirement, freeing up cash from the bank's vault to be lent out with interest.

The other major types of deposit account are transactional(checking) account, money market accounts and time deposit.

types of saving accounts-personal, money market and certificate of deposit

1. **Personal**-Many people save money to cover the cost of unexpected emergencies or to afford a special purchase.

    ☐ **Function-**A personal savings account is an account for a person or persons where depositors earn a rate of interest in return for having restrictions upon how they can access their money. Most savings accounts can be accessed at any time, and many have minimum balance requirements to avoid monthly fees.

    ☐ **Features-**Savings accounts usually come with a passbook or a register that deposits and withdrawals can be recorded in along with interest credits. Banks issue a statement to savings account holders either monthly, quarterly, or semi-annually to provide them with a record of transactions done on the savings account during that period of time.

2. **Money market- A** special type of personal savings account, called a money market, provides account holders with checks that can be written to third parties in a limited number on a monthly basis. Outside of the US, banks provide accounts known as notice deposit accounts, where account holders must notify the institution 90 days before withdrawing money from their savings.

3. Certificate of deposit- A certificate of deposit or CD is a deposit, a financial product offered to consumers by banks and credit unions.

Certificates of Deposit Explained

A certificate of deposit or CD, is an investment instrument entitling the holder to interest payments. Most CDs are issued by banks, insured by the FDIC and include penalties for early withdrawal. They have varying maturity dates and interest rates. The investor profits from the CD by ending up with the original investment plus the sum of the interest payments.

    ☐ **Bank Issuance-**Companies with business operations that exclude banking don't issue CDs. Banks issue CDs as one way to raise money to make loans or invest in other financial instruments that have greater returns, on average, than the CDs used to finance them.

    ☐ **FDIC Insurance-**The Federal Deposit Insurance Commission (FDIC) will insure CDs with certain limitations. They will insure each person's total investment across multiple CDs up to $100,000 for non-retirement and up to $250,000 for retirement funds.

    ☐ **Early Withdrawal-**Bankrate.com states that investors can commonly see early withdrawal penalties equal to six months of interest for removing their funds from a CD before maturity.

There's no legal limit on this penalty, and each bank can set its own policy.

☐ **Maturity Dates-**A CD can last from as short as one month to ten or more years for retirement accounts. Banks usually offer higher interest rates for the longer duration CDs to compensate investors for their extended monetary commitment. Some investors may be tempted to invest in longer duration CDs for the higher rates, especially for retirement CDs, but this incurs the risk of having money tied up for years while interest rates might rise, turning a once-attractive rate into a potential loss when adjusted for rising inflation.

What are the advantages of a certificate of deposit?

Certificates of deposit are a good idea because they are a high interest deposit and offer a higher interest rate than a savings account and treasury bills and notes. CD deposits are less risky than a lot of other investments too.

Disadvantages of a Certificate of Deposit

Certificates of deposit (CDs) are investment vehicles usually offered by banks and savings and loan institutions. They provide the investor a large degree of safety as amounts up to $100,000 are insured by the Federal Deposit Insurance Corporation (FDIC). CDs are purchased in amounts ranging from $500 to $100,000 or more and provide a guaranteed rate of return for a fixed period of time. Although CDs are regarded as safe investments, they do come with certain disadvantages.

1. Limited Liquidity

☐ Certificates of deposit come with a maturity date, which is the point in the future where you receive your original investment plus the accumulated interest. The date could range from several months to even several years into the future. If you attempt to withdraw the money before the maturity date, you will likely be hit with financial penalties, which usually involve being charged for several months' worth of interest. To access your funds without penalty, severe circumstances, such as death or disability, are usually required.

Since your money is effectively tied up, you may miss out on other potentially lucrative investment opportunities that come along.

2. Low Returns

☐ While CDs come with low risk, the return on your investment is also relatively low due to the lower interest rates. Consequently, the amount of interest you earn may not even keep up with the rate of inflation. If high inflation occurs, the effect can be that you actually lose money. You can often earn higher returns over time by investing your money in a mutual fund or the stock market although these investments do not guarantee a return. To get the highest rate of return on CDs, you'll have to invest larger amounts of money over longer periods of time.

3. Tax Disadvantages

☐ Unlike some other investment vehicles, CDs do not offer any tax advantages. With an IRA or 401(k), for example, your money grows on a tax-deferred basis, and you may be able to deduct contributions from your federal taxes. With a CD, you must pay federal, state and local taxes at the time the CD matures. If you're investing in longer-term CDs with higher interest rates, the amount of taxes you owe could be significant.

What Is the Difference Between a Money Market Account & a Savings Account?

you compare money market accounts to savings accounts, you will see that there are quite a few differences. Each account has its advantages and disadvantages. After you review each, you will be able to determine which of these saving accounts will help you meet your goals and objectives. Once you choose an account, you will be required to adhere to the terms and agreements outlined by your financial institution.

Opening Deposit

☐ If you have a savings account, your opening deposit will be somewhere in the area of $50 to $100 depending on the bank. The opening deposit for a money market accounts can be $1,000 to $2,500 depending on the bank.

Withdrawals

☐ With a savings account you can make as many withdrawals or transactions as you would like. If you have a money market account you are limited to three to six transactions per month.

Checks

☐ Savings accounts do not allow you to write checks. Money market accounts allow you to write 3 checks per month.

Interest Rate

☐ The rate of interest on savings accounts can be very low while money market accounts will pay a rate of interest substantially higher.

Minimum Balance

☐ A savings account will have a minimum balance requirement that is much lower than a money market account. The savings account minimum will be approximately $50 and the money market account minimum can be around $500. Requirements vary from bank to bank.

Interest rates

☐ The interest rates on CDs are high compared to other risk-free investments, such as saving accounts, but they are low compared to corporate bonds. Saving accounts have lower interest because they incur no penalties for withdrawal. Bonds have higher interest because they are uninsured and bear the risk of default. CD interest rates are on par with inflation, which is just about 3 percent in the United States

CHECKING ACCOUNTS

A checking account is also known as a transactional account is a deposit account held at a bank or other financial institution, for the purpose of securely and quickly providing frequent access to funds on demand, through a variety of different channels.

Transactional accounts are meant neither for the purpose of earning interest nor for the purpose of savings, but for convenience of the business or personal client; hence do they tend not to bear interest. Instead, a customer can deposit or withdraw any amount of money any number of times, subject to availability of funds.

WHAT IS A CHECKING ACCOUNT NUMBER

Account numbers are generally very useful and efficient file management tools. If a person goes to a bank to open a checking account, she should be given a checking account number. The purpose of this number is to manage transactions that pertain specifically to that customer's transactions. If she needs to make a deposit, she will use her account number so the money can be credited to her and not to someone else. If she needs to withdraw funds, she will need her account number to ensure that she is not taking funds that do not belong to her.

Depending upon the type of account, there can be substantial risk involved in losing or sharing an account number. There are numerous reasons for this. A primary reason is that a customer's file often contains confidential information such as her identity number, credit information, and her home address. Another reason that protection of account numbers is important is because if strangers obtain the numbers, they may gain access to a person's resources, such as her finances.

Features and access

All transactional accounts offer itemized lists of all financial transactions, either through a bank statement or a passbook. A transactional account allows the account holder to make or receive payments by:

ATM cards (withdraw cash at any Automated Teller Machine) Debit card (cashless direct payment at a store or merchant)

- ☐ Cash money (coins and banknotes))
- ☐ cheque and money order(paper instruction to pay)
- ☐ direct debit (pre-authorized debit)
- ☐ Electronic transfers (transfer funds electronically to another account)
- ☐ SWIFT: International account to account transfer.
- ☐ Online banking (transfer funds directly to another person via internet banking facility)
- ☐ Branch- walking into one of your bank locations
- ☐ Internet banking-Internet or online banking describes the use of a bank's secure Web site to view balances and statements, perform transactions and payments, and various other facilities.

Cost to you for having a checking account

Interest rates- paying a low level of interest (money) on your account monthly

Overdrafts-overdraft occurs when the withdrawals from the account exceed the available balance. the fee charged is estimated at \$35-\$50 per transaction

Parents think schools should teach kids about money; schools think it's the parent's responsibility. This means it's rarely taught in school or at home.

All we hear is talk about job. It's not JOBS that set people free...it's teaching kids entrepreneurship and showing them how to be the CEO's of their own lives

CHAPTER 10

INVESTING

The Three Types of Investors

Being an investor is great until you make too many bad choices. Unfortunately there is no secret formula or get rich quick sceems that work or we would all be doing it. The key to financial independence is to focus your energies on a single investing area and dedicate your time to fulfilling your investment vision. We are going to talk about three types of investors, choose one and get to work.

- [ ] **Savers-**A savers primary goal is to invest and wait, they rely on time for their financial independence. They seek low risk growth of their capital and in return will accept, a low rate return. They are working toward retirement and don't want to be bothered with high or low risk investments. They want to play it safe and invest in long term security and retirement. The investments that a saver would usually make are C.O.D'S, 401(K) accounts, mutual funds and diversified investments so that in 30-40 years they have enough to retire and be financially secure. The advantage of being a Saver is that you can spend your time doing other things and not think about investing. The disadvantage is, you have to wait for your financial freedom.

- [ ] **Speculators-** A speculator believes that being in the right place at the right time will pay off. They are looking for the next best investment for them. Unlike Savers, they don't want to rely on time for their financial independance. A Speculator does not concentrate on one specific investment idea or their craft, they kind of go what ever way the wind blows as long as they think there is money to be made. They are somewhat a gambler because they believe that if it doesn't work out this time, there will always be another investment opportunity. While the Speculator has a hot investing edge they often break even or make little profit because they pay so many fees to enter and exit their investments. The advantage of being a Speculator is that you may hit it big if you are in the right place at the right time. The disadvantage is that your returns are so low that you may not make a big return and being a Saver may have worked out better.

☐ **Specialist-**A Specialist Investor relies on education and experience. They believe that being prepared and focusing on a single area of expertise will make you a winner in more ways than one. Most of there investments will be in paper assets, a business owner or in real estate. They will make money if the market is hot or cold because they have a plan. They usually receive huge returns with low risk. It requires the most time and effort but the rewards are more profound because you have control over your income and opportunity for financial success. The advantage of being a Specialist Investor is your plan. If you don't plan, you plan to fail.

There are three types of income:

☐ **Earned- Earned income is generated by working which is based on time/effort spent. It** doesn't matter if you are on salary, hourly, working for someone else or doing your own consulting, it's all considered Earned Income. Jobs, consulting, gambling and owning a small business are all considered Earned income. The advantage of earned income is that you don't need any start up capital, that is why a majority of people choose this income. Another advantage is you can use Earned Income to save up for the other two income brackets which will require less time/effort and more gain. The disadvantages of Earned Income is, if you don't work, you don't get paid. Again it is based on your time and effort. Another disadvantage is that it is taxed at a higher rate than any other income bracket.

- **Portfolio- Portfolio Income is earned by selling an investment at a higher price than you paid for it.** Examples of Portfolio Income is trading paper goods such as stocks and bonds, buying and selling real estate, cars, antiques or any other collectibles that have appreciated in value. The advantage of Portfolio Income is that once you gain enough knowledge and experience you can reinvest or "compound your return" after each sale. If you keep the assets long enough your taxes will be lowered. The disadvantage of Portfolio Income is that you need money to invest upfront and you have little control over your investment because you can not control the sale date or closing on your investment.

- **Passive- Passive Income is money you get from assets you have purchased or created. Passive** Income is generally recurring income month after month or year after year. An example of Portfolio Income is renting a house for more than what your mortgage payment is, a small business that generates income without you working in it, selling and creating intellectual property such as books, patents etc and multi level marketing. The advantages of Portfolio Income is Active control over your investment meaning you have say so in the day-to-day operations, it has favorable tax treatment, such as using your passive income in real estate to take tax deductions in the process and it can be funded through borrowed money such as bank loans as low as 3.5%-20% in real estate.

The bottom line: Specialist investors is the path to financial success but using all three types of income is the path to financial freedom. Using Earned Income is how you start by paying yourself first and generating cash flow(if you are starting from the bottom up). Once you have cash flow you can now move on to Portfolio Income. When it is time to retire you then use your Passive income investments to keep the monthly and yearly income flowing.

What are investments?

INVESTMENTS ARE ASSETS BAGS. There are *fundamental principles of investing* that apply to each of us whether we are seasoned portfolio managers or a novice investor. It never hurts to take time to periodically review these important concepts and improve our foundations upon which we make investment decisions.

Here are 6 fundamental investment principles I use to make myself the best portfolio manager I can be. Notice many of these principles are inter-linked

6 Fundamental Principles of Investing

1. Divide your assets
Studies show that how you divide your assets among asset categories will be the most important determinant of your portfolio returns. This means you should put a maximum effort into asset allocation.

2. Reduce your risk
Asset allocation is the most important form of diversification. But risk can be reduced further by properly diversifying each asset category. Risk that is specific to owning a particular company or industry can be diversified away by owning a variety of non-correlated assets.

3. Be in charge of your money
Whether you manage your portfolio completely on your own, or obtain outside help, make sure you are in charge of your money. Too many people lose everything by trusting someone else with their money. It makes sense to stay in control of your accounts.

4. Compound Growth
Exponential or compound growth is the most powerful principle of investing. The years of compound growth is one of the most important factors in the value of your portfolio. Starting at age 25, a $300 monthly investment earning 8% will build a portfolio of 1 million dollars at age 65. Starting at age 45 will require a $1700 monthly investing for the same outcome.

Reverse compounding can totally devastate a portfolio for many years.

- ☐ If you lose 10% of your portfolio it takes an 11% gain to get back to break even.
- ☐ If you lose 50% of your portfolio it takes a 100% gain to get back to break even.
- ☐ If you lose 70% of your portfolio it takes a 233% gain to get back to break even.

5. Risk Management is crucial

The laws of compounding make risk management a crucial part of investing. If you preserve your capital in a bear market, not only have you not suffered large losses, but you have capital available to invest at much lower prices!

Risk management means purchasing investments with a "margin of safety". Think about what can go wrong with that investment and how badly it would affect the value of that investment. An investor with little debt and lots of cash can better withstand a setback than an investor without these advantages.

6. Have cash available

Most investors buy high and sell low because they let their emotions control their actions. Smart investors buy low and sell for high profits. Market volatility is a fact of investing in the stock market. Always have cash available to buy investments when they are "on sale. This includes real estate, clothes, furniture etc. No one ever goes broke taking large profits.

If you can embrace these fundamental principles of investing you will be miles ahead of the majority of investors. These timeless investment principles can make a gigantic difference in helping you meet your goals and providing the kind of retirement you desire.

3 Different types of investments

1) Owning a business- Owning a business is great but you will pay the cost to be the Boss because it is not an easy task. The **Advantages** that i have found to be true by owning my own salon, Monique Donyale Dominican Salon.com and beauty businesses for over 20 years are;

- [ ] You are the Boss meaning you are in charge of the hiring, firing, operation hours and payroll
- [ ] You get to interactive directly with your clients and create a successful work environment and make a difference in peoples lives through your trade or skill.
- [ ] Nobody can fire you, you are in control of your own destiny.
- [ ] There is a feeling of self satisfaction and accomplishment because you are living to work in a field that you love, not working to live.

SOME DISADVANTAGES ARE

- [ ] **high financial risk in the beginning-**All businesses are not successful the first 3 years. If you can work through the pain and financial burden then you will win later.
- [ ] **No Financial Goals-**Some people don't know when to call it quits. Set a plan of action stating how long you will challenge yourself and if the business is not making a profit, take a break and reinvent yourself. Don't look at it as a failure, look at it as apart of your business development through the school of HARD KNOCKS..
- [ ] **Lawsuits-**You are now pron to lawsuits. Everybody wants what you have but are not willing to work as hard as you are to get it.
- [ ] **Not enough Education-**Most people don't understand that you need more than your skill or trade to own and operate a business. You also need communication skills, marketing and promotion skills, human resource development and life skills to be successful in this endeavor.

10 Qualities of a successful ENTREPRENEUR

☐ **Commitment-To be a boss you must Pledge or promise to have deep involvement in your divine purpose.**

☐ **Discipline-You must** behave in accord with rules of conduct

☐ **Self-Confidence and assertive-**You must feel worthy and know how to express your self-worth when communicating with others.

☐ **Open-Minded-**One must Travel is an ideal way to learn new customs and appreciate different ways of looking at life; but we can't fully appreciate such concepts with a close-mind

☐ **Self-Starter-**A self-starter is a person who takes initiative to solve problems, work without close supervision, and doesn't need to be told what to do on a frequent basis.

☐ **Competitive-** Being inclined, desiring, or suited to compete with others is healthy, but competitive people can provoke feelings of irritation, anxiety, or inadequacy. Learning to deal with it gracefully is a quality you must possess.

☐ **Creativity-**Being able to stimulate the mind will lead to innovative ideas for organization which will create more profitable ideas

☐ **Determination** We learned quickly that the most important predictor of success is determination. Talent is overrated compared to determination, partly because it gives onlookers an excuse for being lazy, and partly because after a while determination starts to look like talent.

☐ **Strong people skills-**people skills – also known as "soft skills" – have as much of an impact on your success as your technical skills. That's especially true when you're in a management or leadership role, you need to apply people skills to achieve your objectives.

☐ **Passion-P**assion is important because without it, it is hard to stay motivated. You need passion to drive you to work harder and harder to learn something. You need passion for what you do to give you the strength to tough out the hard days at work.

2) Real Estate- Is a good investment but it is not for everyone. I am also a real estate investor and what i have learned is that flipping real estate and owning investment property are not the same thing. They both require you to have an interest in the property and the Advantages and Disadvantages are about the same

ADVANTAGES

- ☐ **Profits**-You can make a large profit from selling the real estate you purchase.
- ☐ **Monthly income**-You can also make a profit by keeping the property and using it for monthly rental income
- ☐ **Build Assets and Equity**- If you purchase the right property you will acquire equity. You can use your house as an asset to borrow money from a bank to help you build wealth.

DISADVANTAGES

- ☐ **Tenants don't pay rent**-You will have to take off work to go to court for an eviction and pay the mortgage with your savings
- ☐ **Destroyed property**-When tenants move out, they don't always leave your property in the best condition, which will cost you out of pocket money to repair it, especially if they have lived out there security
- ☐ **Lawsuits**- You may get sued for various reasons and will have to have a lawyer on retainer to handle your cases.

Owning real estate has its perks and drawbacks but I still say owning real estate is definitely one of the avenues to financial freedom.

3) Stock Market-The Stock Market is an exchange place where investors meet to buy and sell shares. A majority of the time the Stock Market have positive returns, but like any other investing there are Advantages and Disadvantages

ADVANTAGES

- ☐ Return on Investment-Great for growing your finances over a period of time.
- ☐ Ownership-You are now a minority owner within a company. When you buy shares, you take an ownership position in the company (although it's relatively small) which allows you to make business decisions in the company. If you know longer want to own your stock, you can sell it to someone else who would like to buy it.

DISADVANTAGES

- ☐ Higher risk- The higher the return, the greater the risk. If the market is down you can loose big or you may not be able to sell your shares
- ☐ Time consuming-Doing the proper research before buying your shares can be time consuming. Not knowing when to exit or sell your shares can also put you at a huge financial disadvantage

One of the primary reasons o invest in the Stock Market is to grow your money. If you can manage your risk, you can invest and take advantage of the Stock Market.

What are stocks and bonds?

Stocks- Stock is the share in an ownership of a company. A claim on the companies assets and earnings. As you acquire stock your ownership in the company becomes greater.

Bonds are a form of a loan or IOU. The holder of the Bond is the lender(creditor), the issuer of the Bond is the borrower(debtor) and the coupon is the interest. Bonds provide the borrower with external funds to finance long term investments.

In a nutshell Stocks represents an ownership in a corporation, Bonds are a form of long term debt in which the issuing corporation promises to pay the principal amount at a specific date. Stocks pay dividends to the owners, Bonds pay interest to the bond holders.

What are IRA'S

The emergence of the IRA as a legitimate retirement investment vehicle affords you the opportunity to reduce your tax burden while saving for the future. Depending on which type of IRA in which you are investing, you may be able to reduce your annual income tax now or you may continue paying taxes on your current income and defer the tax savings until your retirement when you begin receiving disbursements from the IRA account.

5 Types of IRA accounts exist, each with their own benefits or rules.

- ☐ **The original, or traditional IRA**-allows investors to contribute an annual amount and reduce their income tax burden each year they make a deposit.
- ☐ **The Roth IRA** -allows you to contribute an annual amount with the tax savings deferred until you begin taking disbursements upon retirement.
- ☐ **A SEP IRA**- is a traditional IRA the self-employed or small business owners can use in place of a company pension plan.
- ☐ **SIMPLE IRA**- which is similar to a 401(k), except that it is easier for a company to administer--hence the name "SIMPLE."
- ☐ **Self-Directed IRA**- which includes a greater range of investment options, including real estate or business partnerships.

As with any investment, some amount of risk is involved with IRAs, depending on the type in which you are investing. Virtually every financial institution offers IRAs as an investment option and many offer several options from which to choose. You can find IRAs that are low-risk, with stated interest rates, that are similar to long-term certificates of deposit, or you could choose an IRA that will invest your contributions in securities, such as mutual funds, that include a higher level of risk.

Advantages

- ☐ Of course, the obvious benefit to an IRA is the savings you will accumulate over a long period. But don't overlook the tax benefits. Whether you choose to invest in a traditional IRA and keep more of your money from Uncle Sam now, or choose a Roth IRA so you will pay less in taxes when you are on a more fixed income in retirement, the tax savings is by far the No. 1 benefit of any IRA. Some investors have both a traditional and a Roth IRA, so they can enjoy a little of those tax advantages now, and a little more later.

Warning

☐ Early withdrawals from an Individual Retirement Account are taxable, washing away any tax savings you might have enjoyed from making the contribution. Many financial institutions also will tack on an early-withdrawal penalty, as well. Before you contribute to your IRA, make sure you can afford to invest those dollars for the long-term.

What are Mutual Funds?

Mutual funds are investment strategies that allow you to pool your money together with other investors to purchase a collection of stocks, bonds, or other securities that might be difficult to recreate on your own. This is often referred to as a portfolio.

Advantages

☐ **Diversification**-Using mutual funds can help an investor diversify their portfolio with a minimum investment. When investing in a single fund, an investor is actually investing in numerous securities. Spreading your investment across a range of securities can help to reduce risk. This minimizes the risk attributed to a concentrated position. If a few securities in the mutual fund lose value or become worthless, the loss may be offset by other securities that appreciate in value. Further diversification can be achieved by investing in multiple funds which invest in different sectors or categories. This helps to reduce the risk associated with a specific industry or category. Diversification may help to reduce risk but will never completely eliminate it. It is possible to lose all or part of your investment.

☐ **Professional Management**-Mutual funds are managed and supervised by investment professionals, the mutual fund manager will decide when to buy or sell securities. This eliminates the investor of the difficult task of trying to time the market. Furthermore, mutual funds can eliminate the cost an investor would incur when proper due diligence is given to researching securities. This cost of managing numerous securities is dispersed among all the investors according to the amount of shares they own with a fraction of each dollar invested used to cover the expenses of the fund. What does this mean? Fund managers have more money to research more securities more in depth than the average investor.

Now that you know the basics of financing, this should get you started on a very successful journey of becoming financially independent and a responsible adult.

CHAPTER 11

CREDIT –WHAT IS CREDIT?

Sooner or later, almost everyone needs to use credit. Credit lets you use goods and services while you pay for them. Credit is not increased income, it is a way to buy what you can't afford, unlimited, or free.

There are two types of credit loans: personal and business. Personal credit is based on your social security number and business credit is based on your EIN number and reported by Dun and Brad Street

Types of credit

- [ ] **Secured:** With this kind of credit, the creditor guarantees that it will be paid back by putting a lien on an asset you own. The lien entitles the creditor to take the asset if you don't live up to the terms of your credit agreement. Car loans, mortgages, and home equity loans are common types of secured credit.
- [ ] **Unsecured:** When your credit is unsecured, you simply give your word to the creditor that you will repay what you borrow. Credit card, medical, and utilities bills are all examples of unsecured credit.
- [ ] **Installment Credit**
  This is credit that you use to borrow money and promise to repay in equal amounts over a specific period of time.

Example of an installment credit:
Judea signs an auto loan in which he pays the lender $400 each month for five years.

☐ **Revolving Credit**
This is credit that allows you to borrow a per-established amount repeatedly as long as your account is in good standing. You repay the amount borrowed in full or make a partial payment that is subject to interest and/or fees.

Example of revolving credit:
Thomas signs up for a credit card. He uses it to make purchases and at the end of each month, he receives his bill. He can choose to pay off the balance in full or make the monthly minimum payment.

☐ **Open Credit**
This type of credit requires that all money borrowed must be repaid in full every month.

Example of open credit:
Kason has a company charge card he uses to pay all his business expenses. Each month, when he receives the bill, he provides it to the company to pay off the entire balance in full.

Advantages

Like most things, there are advantages and disadvantages to credit cards. Knowing some of these can help you decide if you do or do not want to use credit cards.

☐ **Emergencies**-Sometimes unexpected expenses may occur like your car break down, you need a book for school, help with tuition, your washing machine & dryer break. You can use the credit card to buy or fix these things immediately without having to be inconvenienced but set a goal to pay the bill off in the next two-three months before you make another purchase.

☐ **Building a credit line-** Everything depends on your credit score. Controlled use of a credit card can help you build credit or reestablish your credit but you must pay your bills on time. I recommend having one credit card and only charging 50% of your limit to keep your DTI (DEBT TO INCOME) ratio down. Charging your card to the limit will lower your score

☐ **Don't have to carry cash-** you can use a credit card anywhere and don't have to be concerned with finding an ATM but set a spending limit before you leave the house and stick to it. Over spending will not help your credit but put you in a lot of debt

☐ **vacation-** when you are booking airline tickets and hotel, it is better to use your credit card. If your credit card is stolen, your credit card company will also protect you and fight to delete those charges. In some vacation locations they want you to charge everything to your room so you have to leave your credit card information at check in.

☐ **purchase protection-**if a merchant wont take back a defective product, your credit card company will fight the dispute for you. Check with the credit card company and find out there rules before getting the card

Disadvantages

☐ **Can't afford it-**revolving credit makes it easy to spend beyond your means. If you didn't put it in your budget, then you cant afford it, so don't buy it. Consumers are using credit cards more than ever. If you charge freely you will quickly find yourself in over your head. Young adults are targets for all kind of debt because companies know that at this age you are fighting for your independence and want to keep up with a certain image.

☐ **They will ruin your credit-** If you don't goal set and you use your credit card recklessly, you will be considered a credit risk and can't purchase anything. When it is time to purchase a new house, get an apartment or new car you will be turned down because your DTI (DEBT TO INCOME) ratio is to high which will lower your credit score. Even worst than that, they will give it to you at such a high interest rate that you will have paid for the purchase 5x before you own it.

☐ **high interest rates-**the high interest rates and annual fees associated with credit cards often out weigh the benefits received. This is not FREE MONEY, you have to pay it back and you will pay back 5x the amount you borrowed if it is not paid off within 1-2 months.

The bottom line is that credit cards are only good if you set goals, pay your bills on time or use them in emergency situations. In any other situation CASH IS KING AND KEEPING GOOD BANKING RECORDS.

WHO ARE TRANS UNION, EQUIFAX AND EXPERIAN

The three credit bureaus are simply repositories, or libraries of data where lending agencies report to. It is solely the responsibility of the reporting agency to ensure that the data is correct and NOT the credit bureaus. Mix-ups of credit history's occur when a lender doesn't include pertinent information to differentiate one individual from another. For example, if a lender reports data on one of its borrowers, Bob Smith, and doesn't report it using differentiating data such as address, SS number etc., and the library doesn't recognize which "Bob Smith's" history to affiliate it with.

Essentially, they're three different companies that do the same thing. One thing they all seem to have in common is a propensity for erroneous information on credit reports. Because all three agencies report your credit history slightly differently and because there are errors on a large portion of credit reports, it's recommended to obtain a copy of each, which you can do for free once a year. Bad credit debt normally reports for 7 years before it is taken off your credit report. You can go to a credit repair agency for help but always do your research because all credit repair agencies are legit.

The most efficient way to correct data on your credit report is to dispute it with the credit agency. What happens when you dispute information is the bureau actually sends a notice to the creditor that a specific consumer is disputing the information that the lender is reporting.

The lender then needs to verify and then either change the data or confirm that the data is being reported correctly.

Once that dispute comes back to the bureau, appropriate changes are made or the information remains the same. This is why when the bureau submits the request to the reporting lender/ creditor and the information comes back as being verified, the bureau does not have the permission to change it on your behalf. After the dispute process is completed and you believe that the information is still not correct, my recommendation is to contact the lender directly to dispute with that agency.

SAMPLE DISPUTE LETTER

Date
Your Name
Mailing Address
City, State, Zip

Re: Disputing Inaccuracies on My Credit Report

Name of Credit Reporting Bureau
Mailing Address
City, State, Zip

Dear Sir or Madam:

I am writing for two (2) reasons:

1. To dispute certain information in my credit file; and
2. To have you investigate/re-investigate and remove inaccurate information from my Credit Report and prevent its re-insertion. The item(s) I dispute are encircled on the attached copy of the credit report and further identified by (*identify the items by name of source, such as creditor or tax court, etc. and identify type of item, such as credit account, judgment, etc.*)This item is (inaccurate or incomplete) because (*describe what is inaccurate or incomplete and why*). I am requesting that the item be deleted (*or whatever*

specific change you are requesting) to correct the information.(*If you are enclosing documents such as copies of canceled checks, payment records, court documents, send copies only, you should always retain the originals -- and use the following sentence.*)

Enclosed are copies of the following documents supporting my position:

1.
2.
3.

Please re investigate this (these) matter(s) and (delete or correct) the disputed items within the time frame required by the Fair Credit Reporting Act (FCRA) and inform me in writing of the outcome. Thank you for your time and consideration in this matter.

Sincerely,

_____

(Signature)
Your name

Under the Fair Credit Reporting Act (FCRA, §605A) you can place an initial fraud alert for only 90 days. The credit bureaus will each mail you a notice of your rights as an identity theft victim. Once you receive them, contact each of the three bureaus immediately to request two things:

☐ a free copy of your credit report
☐ an extension of the fraud alert to seven years

You may request that only the last four digits of your Social Security number (SSN) appear on the credit report.

You must have evidence of attempts to open fraudulent accounts and an identity theft report (police report) to establish the seven-year alert. You may cancel the fraud alerts at any time.

What is a FICO sore?

FICO means (Fair Isaac Corporation) and is the credit scoring system used by 90% of the top lenders to summarize credit risk based on a snapshot of a credit report at that particular time. You must understand that every credit score offered on- line is not a FICO score, there are other reporting companies but 90% of lenders use FICO so you should to. FICO scores are based solely on the information obtained by the three credit bureaus. Your score can range from 300-850, the highest being the best. A GOOD CREDIT SCORE IS AROUND 620. Since your credit score is based on your reporting information, you must have atleast 4 open accounts in good standing to base your credit on. If you have nothing reporting you may not have a score which is not good. No credit is just as unhealthy as BAD credit since everything is based on a risk factor and the lenders have nothing to compare it with.

Why a different credit score for each bureau?

Two main reasons:

☐ One is that each bureau uses different scoring models and it evaluates different criteria on the file.

☐ Two is that some creditors or lenders only report to one, two or all three bureaus and in some instances, none of them. It also depends on the information about you on file. Sometimes they may have different information.

Qualifying for Credit

Creditors use information about you and your credit experiences to decide whether or not to give you credit. Your bill-paying history and the number and types of accounts that you have help make this decision. Creditors also use past history on late payments, collection actions, outstanding debt, and the age of your accounts.

A lender will use the five C's of Credit when considering your application for credit:

- ☐ **Character:** Will you repay the debt? How have you paid bills in the past?
- ☐ **Collateral:** What will the lender get if you don't repay the debt?
- ☐ **Capacity:** Can you repay the debt? Do you have adequate income or other available money to pay the debt?
- ☐ **Capital:** What is your net worth? Your net worth is calculated by subtracting your debts from your assets. Assets are items such as money you have and the value of the things you own such as a car or home.
- ☐ **Conditions:** How much money is available in the economy to loan money? When money is tight, interest rates tend to be high.

Here are some tips to help you get credit:

- ☐ Pay all bills on time.
- ☐ Take out a small loan (for example, for a small household appliance or electronic equipment) and pay it off on time.
- ☐ Check your credit report to be sure that your report is complete and accurate.
- ☐ Check that payments you are paying on time each month (such as rent or utility payments) are reported on your credit report.
- ☐ Apply for a secured credit card from a local bank or credit union. To get a secured credit card you must have money in a savings account as collateral. Check to be sure that payments will be reported to your credit report.
- ☐ Don't move or change jobs frequently.
- ☐ Have credit in your own name.

When Should You Use Credit?

Directions: Decide if you think it would be wise to use credit to make these purchases. For each one, put a YES, NO OR MAYBE

Activity

Decide if you think it would be wise to use credit to make these purchases: YES, NO or MAYBE

- [ ] Would you use credit to buy appliances, furniture, or other things for your apartment?
- [ ] Would you use credit to buy gasoline or food?
- [ ] Would you use credit to buy a home or pay for a college education?
- [ ] Would you use credit instead of cash to make several purchases in one store
- [ ] Would you use credit to purchase something that cost $9.99?
- [ ] Would you use credit to purchase something on sale?
- [ ] Would you use credit to pay for a vacation?
- [ ] Would you use credit if you couldn't save enough to buy something you wanted?

ADVICE- don't use credit to purchase small ticket items, you will end up paying more after interest than it originally cost. **USE CREDIT TO BUY BIG PURCHASES LIKE A HOME, CAR ETC** and always set goals to pay it off early.

Know your credit limit

Remember, when you use credit you are using or borrowing someone else's money. Before you accept credit from a lender, you want to think about how much money you can afford to borrow. Too much credit can lead to problems. How do you know if you're using too much credit?

The first step is to add up all your credit by forming two columns. List all of your auto loans, school loans, personal loans, installment loans, and credit card amounts that you usually pay each month in column one titled DEBT. Don't include your mortgage or rent. Put the amount next to it in column two TITLED AMOUNT.

Activity

Credit and Miscellaneous break down

Divide your total monthly debt payment by your monthly take-home pay. (DEBT / INCOME= X 100)

For example: If your monthly take-home pay is $1100 and total monthly debt payment is $132 then your debt rate is 12%

$132 ÷ $1100 = $0.12
0.12 X 100 = 12%

- **What is your total monthly debt payments?**
- **What is your monthly take home pay?**
- **What is your debt rate?**

Now, compare your debt rate from above. Do you have too much credit debt?

How Are You Doing?

Percentage
Do you have too much credit debt?

10 percent
Congratulations! Like 85% of all American families you limit the amount of debt you carry on your credit cards.

11 to 15 percent
You are in the high average group. Don't be too alarmed but you should slow down and try to get your debt closer to 10%.

16 to 20 percent
You have more debt than most people with your income. Only five out of 100 people owe as much as you do. Start working on reducing your debt.

21 to 25 percent
RED ALERT! Your home, your car, and your debt are probably eating up 75% of your paycheck. It's time for a dramatic change. You may need help from the National Foundation for Credit Counseling (1-800-388-2227) or Myvesta.org.

26 percent or more

You definitely have far more credit than you can handle. You need professional help immediately to reduce your debt. Start by calling the agency below.

Monthly Budget Example;

Here is an example of how the break down of your monthly budget should be so you stay on track: Start with 100% of your monthly income

Mortgage(apartment rent etc)- 25%
Transportation-15%
utilities-10%
food-10%
clothing-5%
medical-10%
personal-5%
entertainment-5%
miscellaneous-5%
Pay yourself first(save)-10%

You may have to shuffle the numbers around a little but i hope this helps

Needs -vs- Wants

Before you can determine your Needs and Wants, you have to know your Values. Values are influenced by things and persons that have touched your life. Your values are influenced by your parents, family, friends, church, community and schools. Some values may be, paying your bills on time, goal setting, education, paying your tides at church, owning a home, buying a reliable car, being an entrepreneur or you may have been taught to work hard and follow your dreams. Whatever your desires, they will show up in what you decide your NEEDS -VS- WANTS will be.

Lets define Needs and Wants

- **Needs** are things that we require to live. Examples- food, water, shelter
- **Wants** are extra's that make our lives more enjoyable and comfortable to live. We can do without them if we don't have the money to buy it. Examples- designer pocketbooks, CD's, 50 pair of shoes or sneakers, designer clothes, the spa, designer watches, motorcycles, eating out. You get the point.

Now lets be CLEAR, I'm not saying not to buy your WANTS, I'm just saying you should set goals and budget so you don't get evicted or have your lights turned off to look good because sitting on the curb or living in the dark is no fun. Don't hustle backwards because having something and loosing it is worst than never having it at all.

What is identity theft?

Identity theft is a form of stealing someone's identity in which someone pretends to be someone else by assuming that person's identity, typically in order to access resources or obtain credit and other benefits in that person's name. The victim of identity theft (here meaning the person whose identity has been assumed by the identity thief) can suffer adverse consequences if they are held accountable for the perpetrator's actions. Identity theft occurs when someone uses another persons identifying information, like their name, identifying number, or credit card number, without their permission, to commit fraud or other crimes.

What to do if you are a victim of IDENTITY THEFT

Notify credit bureaus and establish fraud alerts. Immediately report the situation to the fraud department of the three credit reporting companies -- Experian, Equifax, and Trans Union. When you notify one bureau that you are at risk of being a victim of identity theft, it will notify the other two for you. Placing the fraud alert means that your file will be flagged and that creditors are required to call you before extending credit. Consider using your cell phone number for faster notification.

Equifax:P.O. Box 740250, Atlanta, GA 30374- 0241.
Report fraud: Call (888) 766-0008 and write to address above.
TDD: (800) 255-0056
Web: www.equifax.com
Experian:PO Box 9532
Allen TX, 75013
Report fraud: Call (888) EXPERIAN (888-397-3742) and write to address above.
TDD: Use relay to fraud number above.
Web: www.experian.com/fraud
TransUnion:P.O. Box 6790, Fullerton, CA 92834-6790.
Report fraud: (800) 680-7289 and write to address above.
TDD: (877) 553-7803
E-mail (fraud victims only): fvad@transunion.com
Web: www.transunion.com

SAVING AND ESTABLISHING GOOD CREDIT

Organizations, credit unions, and resources that can assist with saving options and establishing good credit.

AnnualCreditReport.com
Offers a free credit report, once every 12 months from each of the nationwide consumer credit reporting companies: Equifax, Experian, and TransUnion free of charge.
https://www.annualcreditreport.com

Bankrate, Inc.
Provides financial rate information, offering rate data, and financial content.
www.bankrate.com/

Consumer Credit Counseling
Provides comprehensive financial counseling, education, and helps consumers achieve financial independence through debt reduction, home ownership, and improved money management skills.
https://www.cccssf.org/

Federal Trade Commission's Identity Theft Resources

Provides detailed information to help deter, detect, and defend against identity theft.

www.ftc.gov/bcp/edu/microsites/idtheft/

National Foundation of Credit Counseling

Provides free and low-cost help from a trained, certified counselor who will assist you in determining the best options to meet your individual needs.

www.nfcc.org

Youth Credit Union Network

Serves the youth constituency.

www.cdcu.coop/i4a/pages/index.cfm?pageid=285

After you have decided what's most important to you, set some short and long term goals. Goals are what you hope and plan to achieve in the future. They are something to work for. They are different than dreams or "New Year's Resolutions." Now that you know a little bit about credit, use your credit responsibly. It can help you but also hurt you.

CHAPTER 12

TAXES

IRS

U.S. Internal Revenue Service (IRS)
Federal income and payroll taxes specifically business and self-employed taxpayers.
www.irs.gov/ or 800-829-4933

The IRS is owned and organized by the United States government. This organization is not owned by any one individual. It is completely controlled by the government. The IRS is responsible for collecting taxes and the interpretation and enforcement of the Internal Revenue Code

☐ **Why do We Pay Taxes?** We pay taxes because it's the law and it helps to provide services in our community. Every year around April 15 all tax information must be turned in to the government. If the government took out to much money during the year, you will receive a TAX REFUND. If you didn't pay taxes through out the year(this usually applies to self-employed citizens) you will be required to pay them at this time. Most employees will start receiving their W2 at the end of January and can file for their TAX REFUND. Paying taxes is apart of our civic duty, it is also the law. If you don't pay your taxes you may have to pay penalties or go to jail.

Our tax dollars also go toward;

- ☐ social security
- ☐ Medicare
- ☐ to maintain safe roads
- ☐ funds public libraries and parks
- ☐ funds government programs to help the less fortunate
- ☐ schools
- ☐ support the salaries of judges, legislators, police and fire fighters and more
- ☐ salaries of government workers.

Why do We Pay Sales Tax?

We pay sales tax as a way to support the local governments in our states. The money is used to fund public parks and schools, and to pay the wages of state workers.

Why do We Pay Federal Taxes?

We pay federal taxes to support the federal government. Our taxes go to things like military budget, government programs, and to pay politician's salaries.

What is F.I.C.A? You may have seen the acronym FICA on your paycheck but do not know what it stands for. FICA stands for Federal Insurance Contributions Act, and in exchange for a certain percentage withheld from your paycheck, you are eligible for Social Security and Medicare. While you may not like to have the amount taken out of your account, it is a tax every employee has to pay. Consequently, it's a good idea to understand how to determine if you're exempt from paying it.

Should you be paying FICA as a student? Obtain proof that you are a student. As of 2004, students enrolled full time in an accredited college program are exempt from paying FICA taxes. Contact your student financial aid administrator for the latest information.

- Check with your employer or your local Social Security office by visiting socialsecurity.gov. It is not uncommon for tax laws to change with the political tides, so if you're in doubt about your FICA exemption status, set up an interview with your employer or the Social Security office.

Self-employed tax forms vs Employee tax forms

A W2 is the form employee's use, while 1099 Miscellaneous forms are for Self-employed people.

☐ Self-employed freelancers must also pay the entire FICA portion (Social Security and Medicare) of their taxes. "You do get a credit for paying part of it, but you still have to pay it out-of-pocket. There are also state and local taxes to be paid, which require more forms, along with 1099s, that have to be filled out *four times* a year. Most of the pay as a Self-Employed person varies from month to month

☐ With a W2, most taxes are cut and dry. The employer pays half the FICA portion, and the potential for making a mistake is much smaller. "The W2 is spelled out "and most of the pay is regular." there is only one form to look out for at the end of the year.

Make sure you pay your taxes or the I.R.S will be on your tail

CHAPTER 13

APARTMENT RENTAL 101

How does my credit history affect me getting an apartment?- Many landlords base your credit history and your debt on your ability to pay your rent on time. A good score is around 620. If you are looking in a nice area with a high demand and a good school system and there are more tenants looking for an apartment than apartments available, they may look for a score of 700. In lower income areas you may find a cheaper apartment that requires a lower credit score but safety may be a concern so be mindful and be safe.

Prepare a good response to bad credit history

Landlords are people to and you can explain why you had a rough patch and fell behind.

- ☐ you became ill or temporary lost your job. If they don't understand, then maybe you wouldn't want to be their tenant anyway.
- ☐ You can offer to pay a higher security deposit
- ☐ pay 6 months rent upfront

How do I find a safe location- people move for many reasons jobs, schools, transportation, family, financial reasons, kitchen, the view, size, the exterior structure and much more. When you find that it is time to relocate here are some things to help you out;

- ☐ **Plan ahead-** Start looking a month or two in advance. This will also give you time to give ample notice to your landlord if you are already out on your own. Never burn your bridge because you may need to use the old landlord as a reference. Planning ahead also eliminates taking the first available apartment even if you don't want it.

- ☐ **Fancy word games-** Look out for word like cozy which means comfortable but they could mean small or Unique which means different but it could mean different in a weird way. Remember the landlords job is to get you to the location and get a good tenant.

- ☐ **The pressure trap-**Don't fall for the sales pitch "I have 10 other people interested so you have to let me know now and leave a non refundable deposit if your serious". That may or may not be true about the other people but don't get scammed out of your deposit. Do your homework and find out through city hall if the person you are talking to is the owner. If its a Realtor or agent make sure they are who they say they are. Always ask for I.D..your job is to find a good safe location for you.

- ☐ **Intuition-**If the location doesn't feel good to you then don't move there. Most leases are for one year and you don't want to be unhappy that long.

Filling out the lease

When filling out an apartment lease ask if it is for one year or month-to-month. A yearly lease requires you to stay for one year before you can move or renew your lease. A month-to-month lease means at the end of a given month you can move. This type of lease is good for a temporary stay or someone waiting to close on a house or about to relocate. If you have a roommate you both should be present when filling out the required information.

Most leases are standard or they may have a rider attached. A Rider is an attached document which will now become apart of the legal binding contract(lease) with other rules for the rental. When reviewing or signing a lease look for these things;

- ☐ Amount of security deposit(usually month and half of rental space)
- ☐ Monthly rental amount
- ☐ Term of lease(one year or month-to-month)
- ☐ Rules
- ☐ Read The fine print
- ☐ Do a walk through before you move in and after you move out. Always leave your apartment clean. Take before and after pictures, print them and keep them in your file. This will eliminate any doubt about the landlord not returning your security deposit or accusing you of ruining there apartment.
- ☐ Make sure information on Lead is provided with your lease. Check your state for more information

Some required documents are; always use copies if required to leave information

- ☐ I.D.
- ☐ References (usually three)
- ☐ Social Security card
- ☐ Verification of employment(pay stub)

How can I make breaking a lease easier?

We all know that life happens and plans may not always go accordingly so you need to prepare and EXIT strategy. Breaking a year lease is never easy for anyone, especially the landlord since he has added the rent into his monthly expense budget. Here are some tips to make it easier for both parties;

- ☐ If you suspect that you can not stay a year, ask if a month to month lease is an option. If not, then maybe you should not move there because it can cause a bad debt to be reported on your credit which will make it challenging to rent another apartment when you are ready.
- ☐ Give proper notice-The minute you are aware that you may have to leave early, inform your landlord. The landlord has the right to sue you for the remainder of the lease if you cannot work out an agreement
- ☐ sublease- ask if subleasing is an option. Subleasing is when you allow someone else to live there while paying the rent but the lease is still in your name until the end of the term.

What is a security deposit?

A security deposit is the money a landlord takes from a tenant that is not apart of the monthly rent. The reason for the security deposit is to assist in repairs if you (the tenant) damages the apartment. It can also be used as last months rent if stated in the lease. There are limits to how much a security deposit can be, check with your state or Google it.

After moving in you should receive a statement from your landlord showing you what interest bearing or dividend yielding account your deposit is in. If this is not done with in 30 days you must give the landlord written notice to comply with the statue(law). If the landlord still does not comply, you have the right to use your security deposit for your rent and never have to give another security deposit as long as you live in that apartment and the landlord can not ask you to do so, according to the state of New Jersey, Security Deposit law (#5) pursuant to section 2 of P.L. 1967, c. 265 (C. 46:8-20) Check the laws for your state under security deposit.

In most states a landlord has up to 30 days to return your deposit. If a landlord do not want to return your full deposit you can file a claim in small claims court and have proof of why you are owed your money and take your pictures. If the landlords argument is that you have done damage to the apartment, he must have receipts showing the repair amount.

Things to Consider When Finding a Roommate

Finding the perfect roommate can seem like an impossible mission. The key is communication to determine if your next roommate is right for you.

Follow the Q&A below to help you decide.

1) Question-Were you already acquainted with this person?

Your Answer- Yes, we've met, or he/she is a total stranger

My answer- Find out more information about this person

Your answer-yes, we are BFF

My answer- be careful. If your already girlfriends, the relationship can get rocky when you're roommates. If your friend is bossy and manipulate and have a different lifestyle from you.

WARNING-DO NOT LIVE WITH THIS PERSON!!

2) Question- Do you have similar sleep patterns?

Your answer-Yep! Or No, one's a night owl; the others an early riser.

My answer- keep asking questions

Your answer- the two parties are willing to work around each others schedule

My answer- If you are willing to compromise then it's OK. If not you will constantly will be bothering each other and end up trying to break the lease.

WARNING- DO NOT LIVE WITH THIS PERSON!

3) Question-Are you both nonsmokers?

Your answer-Yep! Or no, we both smoke

My answer- continue on with your questioning

Your answer- one of us smoke and the other does not

My answer- can you come up with some smoking ground rules. Some of the person's lifestyle choices don't match your own preferences. If not

WARNING- DO NOT LIVE WITH THIS PERSON!

4) Question- Do you both drink socially? What about your social life?

Your answer-Yes, occasionally or one drinks and the other does not

My answer-additional question time

Your answer- one of us like to party but the other like's quiet nights in

My answer- Whoa, could be trouble, be sure to ask: it's important for you to have similar social lifestyles with your roommate. If your roommate is looking for a BFF and you already have two the Contrasting personalities could become exhausting if their looking to bond or spend time with you. If they have three boyfriends and you r a one man type of girl, be careful

Your answer- She/ he is bisexual

My answer- different sexual preferences could lead to destruction if not handled with caution.

WARNING- DO NOT LIVE WITH THIS PERSON!

5) Question-Did you get a good first impression?

Your answer- Yeah, the person seemed nice / responsible or the person was late and disrespectful

My answer-OK, maybe you have a roommate, but if they were rude and disrespectful They may not respect deadlines, which could lead to late bill paying.

Your answer- They were not neat looking

My answer- Ask questions but be careful because they could be a slob. Worst yet, they are a neat freak and you are a slob. This kind of different behavior is often about being organized and unorganized which could drive you crazy.

WARNING- DO NOT LIVE WITH THIS PERSON!

6) Question-Will the person give you previous roommate references?

Your answer-yes, I'm calling now or no that's weird. Because they have never lived on their own before

My answer-If the references check out, you have found roommate material. If they have no references This could be a red flag that the person hasn't been a great roommate in the past. You could always ask their parents but be careful because they may just want them out of there house. Lol!

Conclusion:

Make sure to consider all of your roommate requirements and preferences before starting your search. Then, ask any questions you feel are necessary to determine whether or not this person would make a good roommate.

After all, you'll have to live with him or her, so do what you can to ensure it will be an enjoyable experience for the both of you.

Frequently asked questions

Q: <u>Does everyone that I am going to live with need to fill out an application?</u>
A: Yes. It gives the landlord the information they need to conduct a background and reference check and must be filled out completely and truthfully. We will review income/employment, rental history, credit/payment history, and criminal history.

Q: <u>Is there a fee to apply?</u>
A: Yes, if owned by a corporation, most private owners do not require one. Payment of the fee does not guarantee approval.

Q: <u>Does everyone that is going to live in the apartment need a co-signer for the lease?</u>
A: It depends. Some require a signed co-sign agreement form for each applicant under the age of 21 in order to sign a lease. Applicants age 21 and over may not be required to obtain a co-signer but must meet stricter income/employment, rental history and credit score standards.

Q: <u>After I submit my application/fee and signed co-sign agreement form, what happens next?</u>
A: Once the landlord received and approved applications and co-sign forms for everyone who will be living in the apartment, he will set up a time to give you the keys

Q: <u>If I co-sign for an applicant, am I responsible for the other roommates as well?</u>
A: Some leases are written so that all lessees are "jointly and severally" liable. This means they are individually and collectively responsible for the terms and conditions of the lease. Even though you are co-signing for just one person, you are responsible for the other roommates through joint and several liability.

Q: <u>Can I see a sample copy of a lease I would be signing?</u>
A: Yes. A sample lease should be available for you to review before signing.

Q: <u>Can two people share a bedroom?</u>

A: Yes if permitted by City housing code. It will also costs additional rent per month for each additional tenant on the lease. For example, if 5 tenants lease a four-bedroom apartment, or 2 tenants lease a one-bedroom apartment, there will be an additional $100(or agreed upon amount) rent charged per month. All people living in an apartment must be listed on the lease.

Q: <u>When do leases begin and end?</u>

A: Leases begin at the beginning of each month or on the 15th and end 12PM the following year, unless it is a month to month lease.

Q: <u>Is subleasing allowed?</u>

A: It is up to the landlord. If you choose to sublease, you are responsible for finding a new renter. The new renter must fill out a rental application, obtain a co-signer if necessary, and be approved by the landlord and all other roommates/tenants listed on the lease prior to moving in. It is important to remember that when you sublease, your obligations under your original lease are not terminated. If the person to whom you sublease fails to meet any of the lease obligations (rent payment, damages, unpaid utilities, etc.) you may be held liable.

Q: <u>How much is the security deposit and when is it due?</u>

A: The security deposit is equal to one month's rent and it is due when you sign your lease.

Q: <u>When is rent due? When is it considered late?</u>

A: Your first month's rent payment will be collected when you sign your lease. For subsequent months' rent is always due on the first day of the month, even if it falls on a holiday or weekend. Sometime you will get a 5 day grace period.

Q: <u>Can we write more than one check each month to pay our rent?</u>

A: Sometime it is accepted, again it depends on the landlord.

Q: <u>Can I get a satellite dish at my apartment?</u>
A: Most of the time it is excepted as long as the satellite company can install it.

Q: <u>Do you allow dogs or cats at your properties?</u>
A: Always check your lease because if they are not allowed you can face possible eviction for breach of contract. Designated service animals are permitted with proper documentation and disability verification.

Always read the fine print and ask questions. Know what the penalties are for late return and/or damage, and double-check them with someone in person

What can I do if the landlord won't make repairs in my apartment?

One thing you cannot do is not pay your rent to get revenge on the landlord. This is not a good defense if the landlord takes you to court for eviction. The judge will just think that you did not have the money. Consult with legal aid, it's usually free and they are located in or near your city hall.

Here are some tips;

- ☐ Put your complaint in writing- Always try to work it out first
- ☐ inform city hall and have an inspector come out
- ☐ Take your landlord to court- File a Warranty of Habitability claim, which is a defense to non-payment of rent where conditions are dangerous to life, health or safety,". Have nice clear photos printed out to help your defense
- ☐ Do it yourself- Get an estimate and hire a contractor to do the job. Deduct it from your rent and send the receipt

What does it mean to have an income based apartment

Income

- ☐ Income restricted apartments rent only to individuals who meet certain income requirements. Since income restricted housing is designed to benefit those with low to middle incomes, the income requirement consists of a maximum, instead of a minimum like other apartments. Individuals and families who pay more than 30 percent of their income for housing, as determined by the average income of the area in which they live, are considered cost burdened and are most likely to qualify for income restricted housing.

Housing

☐ To be designated as income restricted, or affordable housing, an apartment building must offer apartments at rates that are less than the fair market value in the area. Likewise, the rent must not exceed 30 percent of the adjusted gross income of an individual or family whose income is equal to 65 percent of the areas median income. The apartment must also have at least 20 percent of its units occupied by low income individuals, and must accept section 8 housing vouchers.

How do I find out the landlord tenant laws in my state?

Knowing the landlord tenant laws in the state you will be living is an important thing to look into prior to actually securing an apartment, especially if this will be your first rental. The laws in every state have been enacted to lay the groundwork for an informed relationship between the two parties and can vary from place to place. Many of these details are spelled out in a document called a lease.

Landlords will often protect their rights by doing things such as a credit check and contacting former landlords or references given by the potential renter. This can help them to make sure a person will be a responsible tenant.

Those who are looking for an apartment will want to carefully evaluate the lease agreement to make certain they understand what will be expected of them, and that they can fulfill those obligations. The time to investigate tenant rights and responsibilities is before signing the lease and moving into a particular property.

Most landlords are already aware of the laws that outline the rental relationship in their state. Those looking to rent an apartment may want to check out the laws on the Internet before beginning their search, especially if they are a new arrival to the area.

HOW TO FURNISH YOUR APARTMENT

10 Tips for Apartment Decorating

- ☐ remove or add carpet
- ☐ personalize your linen
- ☐ Add an area rug
- ☐ use a fresh coat of paint
- ☐ Add mirrors
- ☐ Add throw pillows or chair covers
- ☐ window treatments
- ☐ Add pictures
- ☐ Change your kitchen appliances
- ☐ Hang plants

Cleaning your apartment

You should schedule to clean your apartment or home at least once a week depending on how many people reside in the home. Cleaning your residence should consist of;

- ☐ The bathroom- use bleach to sanitize the toilet, sinks and mop the floor
- ☐ The kitchen- never leave dishes in the sink over night. Keep the table and counters clean to prevent bugs and always sanitize your dish drain and mop the floor
- ☐ Living & dining room- dust the tables and vacuum or mop the floor
- ☐ bedrooms- Make up your bed daily so you can come home to an organized room. This will help you to relax after a long day

Make cleaning your home a team effort. Everybody should have a choir to do and it would work better if all cleaning was done within 24 hours apart, depending on everyone's work and school schedule.

What Are the Benefits of a Post Office Box?

Post office boxes are available through most United States Postal Service (USPS) locations. These boxes provide numerous benefits to customers, from their 24/7 availability to privacy protection and more

Availability-At most USPS offices, post office boxes are in an an area of the facility that's always open, so you can pick up your mail any time, day or night.

Security-Locked post office boxes are built into an interior wall of the USPS location, accessible only by postal workers and owners of the boxes. As an additional security measure, only one unique key is provided to the box owner (to be replaced only if lost).

Stability-No matter how often you move, your post office box address remains the same and you never need to miss mail with change of addresses.

Convenience-If you leave on vacation, or travel on business, your mail is held for you at your post office box, ready to be picked up when you're ready.

Privacy Protection-Putting your private home address on forms, applications, Internet orders and so on compromises your privacy because the address can be added to search able databases, mailing lists and other publications without your knowledge. By using a post office box address instead, you safeguard your private home address.

What is Rent to Own?

Rent to own means exactly what it says. Rent to own is a way to buy or sell something over time, giving the buyer an "option" to purchase at some point in the future. This is an alternative way to buy a house. A rent to own transaction, also known as a lease option, starts with the contract. Both the buyer and seller agree to certain terms, and all of the terms can be changed to fit everybody's needs. At the beginning of any rent to own transaction, the buyer pays the seller an "Option Premium," which is often around five percent of the ultimate purchase price (it can certainly be higher or lower). This gives the buyer an option to purchase the house, not an obligation. The "Option Premium" is non refundable. that means if you change your mind about purchasing the house, you do not get your money refunded. The Seller keeps your deposit. This compensates the seller for waiting around(1-5 years) to see what the buyer will do. After all the seller can not sell the home to anybody else while he is under contract with the buyer.

Monthly payments-The buyer/renter also makes monthly payments to the seller. Those payments serve as rent payments (because the seller still owns the property), but the renter typically pays a little bit extra each month. The additional amount is usually credited to the final purchase price, so it reduces the amount of money the buyer has to come up with when buying the home.

Advantages of Rent to Own-There are perks to using this method of home buying. Here are a few tips;

- ☐ It gives you time to repair your credit and save up for a larger down payment.
- ☐ You get to live in the house first and learn all of the responsibilities of being a home owner
- ☐ you get to learn about the house. You get a pretty good idea of how much the utilities will cost and outside maintenance

Disadvantages

- ☐ **Forfeit your Option Premium**-if you don't buy, you loose your deposit
- ☐ **Foreclosure**- the seller could stop paying the mortgage and loose the house. That means you loose everything to.
- ☐ **The market could drop**-If you have agreed on a purchase price and now the house is not worth that price anymore 5 years from now, a bank won't loan you money to buy a house that does not have the value. Unless you can buy it in cash, you're stuck.
- ☐ **Title problems**- Get a title search and inspection done as if you where purchasing the home. Title problems will prevent you from purchasing the home

Sellers risk of rent to own

- ☐ No certainty: Your renter might not buy, so you have to start all over again and find another buyer or renter (but at least you get to keep the extra money)
- ☐ Slow money: You don't get a large lump-sum, which you might need to purchase your next house.
- ☐ No conceit deal: You typically lock in a sales price when you sign a rent to own agreement, but home prices might rise faster than you expected. You might do better renting the place and getting a sales agreement in the future (or you might not).
- ☐ Market decrease: Home prices might fall, and if your renter does not buy, you would have been better off simply selling the property.

Getting your own apartment is pretty exciting. Just be aware of people trying to take advantage of your kindness and move in without paying bills. Always set boundaries and be clear on what you expect from your roommate or partner.

CHAPTER 14

PURCHASING A HOME

Purchasing a home

Owning a home requires a tremendous commitment of funds, time, and attention.

The following topics should help make your decision a little easier: **The most important thing to consider when buying a home is a great mortgage company who can close the deal**. A Realtor can always be of great assistance in finding the home of your dreams. Owning a home is not for everyone, some people rather not assume the responsibility it involves or they just may not want to be tide to a thirty years financial commitment. Owning a home definitely has some advantages and disadvantages. Here are a few tips;

Advantage of purchasing a home

- ☐ **There is pride in owning your home**- Being a home owner is an investment. It makes you feel good to see your vision come to life
- ☐ **Tax deduction**-The interest and property tax portion of your mortgage payment is a tax deduction.
- ☐ **increase in value**- the longer you own your home, the equity increases which means your money value increase
- ☐ **security**- Owning a home ties you to your community, making it more difficult to suddenly pick up and leave a location.

- [ ] **you are paying yourself-** you can borrow against your equity as you pay down your mortgage or your property increase in value
- [ ] **design to your liking-** No landlord to ask, you are in charge and can make any improvements to your home at anytime.
- [ ] **more space-**You can have more space or just as much in your home and pay almost the same price as renting an apartment. Most of the time you can have a driveway or garage if you choose to.

Disadvantages of purchasing a home

- [ ] **Commitment- Home ownership** is a long-term financial commitment.
- [ ] **Down payment-** Buying a home requires a down payment(3.5% FHA or 20% commercial), closing costs and moving expenses.
- [ ] **Repairs-** You must have money saved for unexpected repairs, for example the furnace or water heater may break.
- [ ] **Property taxes-** depending on where and what state you purchase your home, your property taxes can really increase your mortgage payment

What is the process of purchasing a home?

The home buying process is not as scary as it may seem. Here is the process in a nut shell.

- [ ] **Get pre-approved by a mortgage company-**Don't start looking for a home until you have been approved so that you will know what price range you can afford. If you are a first time home buyer, more than likely you will get an FHA loan. If you already own a home and your purchasing a second home you will go conventional because you can only have one FHA loan at a time.
- [ ] **Decision process-** Now you have to decide what kind of home you are looking for. Do you want a three or four bedroom, small or large kitchen, dining and living room, how many bathrooms, do you want a ranch style or colonial house, a yard, driveway, basement etc

☐ **Shopping process**- Either a Realtor or investor will gather a list of properties based on your description and you will go see the inside of each one and narrow it down to your dream home.

☐ **Closing the deal**- Once you have selected your home it is now time to close the deal. This process usually takes anywhere from 30-60 days depending on how fast you provide the loan officer with the needed documents required to close a deal..

☐ **You are now a NEW HOME OWNER, enjoy your investment!!!!**

What is a FHA, Conventional and VA Mortgage?

☐ **An FHA loan** is a mortgage insured by the Federal Housing Administration. Borrowers with FHA loans pay for mortgage insurance, which protects the lender from a loss if the borrower defaults on the loan. This is for first time home buyers. With this loan the property must be owner occupied, so you can only have one at a time. This type of loan require a 3.5% down payment.

☐ **A conventional mortgage** refers to a loan that is not insured or guaranteed by the federal government. A conventional, or conforming, mortgage adheres to the guidelines set by Fannie Mae and Freddie Mac. It may have either a fixed or adjustable rate. This loan requires a 20% down payment and is used by people purchasing investment properties or a second home.

☐ **A VA loan** is a mortgage loan in the United States guaranteed by the U.S. Department of Veterans Affairs (VA). The loan may be issued by qualified lenders. The VA loan was designed to offer long-term financing to eligible American veterans or their surviving spouses (provided they do not remarry). Some of these programs require a 0% down payment

Documents you need to purchase a home?

Here are a few questions that a loan officer will be asking you when purchasing a home:

1) Do you know your credit score? They will run it themselves anyway
2) Job history should be two years- will need to show pay stubs

3) If you were not on the same job for two years but where in the same field for two years that's acceptable

4) Must have two years w2 or 1099

5) How much do you make yearly?

6) Social security card and copy of driver's license for ID

7) Rent receipts for one year. (There are exceptions that loan officers can make)

8) Do you have a house loan already?
   If so is it FHA or conventional?

9) What type of house are you looking for-(one family etc)

10) What city?

11) Do you have cash reserves (money in the bank for a down payment and closing cost? If not will someone be gifting you the down payment?

What is a Mortgage down payment?

Down payments are expressed in percentages such as 3.5%(FHA) or 20% (Conventional). The down payment is money that goes to the seller when purchasing a house, the rest comes from your mortgage payments. Your down payment can come from your saving, money received from an investment or gifts an grants from family or non profit organizations. A GIFT is money that a family member or friend gives to you for a down payment, that do not have to be paid back.

What are closing cost?

More than likely home buyers will pay about 2 to 5 % of the purchase price of their home in closing fees. So, if your home cost $100,000, you might pay between $2,000 and $5,000 in closing costs. This is in addition to the down payment

Safety first

- ☐ Make sure you have a fire extinguisher
- ☐ carbon monoxide detector
- ☐ smoke alarms
- ☐ electrical socket covers

Buying a home will be one of the biggest purchases you make. When choosing a home, be true to yourself and your life style. If you are looking to purchase a home go to BuyRetailProperties.com They help you find a home below market value, help with closing cost and can close within 30-45 days after you find the property

Chapter 15

Purchasing a Car

The time has come and you want to buy a car but you don't know where to start. There are so many cars and dealerships to choose from. Here are some tips to help you get started

Tips for buying the right car for you

- ☐ **Set a budget-** having a goal of your spending limit will keep you focused on what you can afford instead of what you want. Decide if you will do a cash purchase or a car loan using a down payment and pay a monthly car note

- ☐ **Decide on a car type-** What car will fit into your budget that require low cost maintenance. Don't buy a BMW if you cant afford to pay for the oil change, maybe to start out you should get a Ford focus or a small Honda.

- ☐ **New or used-** There are good used cars for sale. Make sure the miles match the year of the car and get a warranty you choose a new car, make sure that you get a good deal and ask about rebates

- ☐ **Shop around for a lender-** Do your homework, use Bankrate's rate search tool to find out the interest rates nationwide before you arrive at he dealer. Check credit unions and local lenders --vs- conventional banks for lower interest rates.

- ☐ **Negotiate starting at wholesale or below sticker price-** Go to a third party car site and type in the exact car that you want, include everything like color, trim, year, sunroof etc. Print out the page and start your negotiations from there. With a new car go a little above sticker price. With a used car start at wholesale price. After you have gotten the sales person to commit to a number, **then and only then** do you tell him about your cash back rebates, incentives or dealer discounts. If you tell the sales person before hand, he will only raise the purchase price then add in the discount leaving you getting nothing

- **Check car history-** Check the vehicle model Reliability Rating to get an estimate cost of repairs and how often you will have to get it serviced. For used cars, i recommend asking for a CARFAX. You can go to CARFAX.com and do it yourself

- **Be aware of dealer financing-** Be aware of good deals that are to good to be true, especially if your credit is less than perfect. Most dealerships will receive a commission if they can get you to go through them for the car loan so they really are not concerned with getting you the best rate. Dealers will tell you that they can get you good rates but they forget to tell you that it is contingent on the loan approval. These situations can lead to the dealership asking for a larger down payment, higher interest rates or in some cases you have to return the car if you won't comply after you have driven it home and had if for a couple of days thinking it is now your car..

- **Ask about rebates-** Visit third party sites and the dealer sites for incentives, cash rebates etc, for veterans, college students and first time buyers. You must ask for these discounts or you won't get them. Always have THE DISCOUNTS ready to show on your phone or a print out

- **Factor in your trade in-** Do the same negotiating when using a trade in. Research your cars worth on a third party site and print it out. If asked about a trade in, just say you are not sure. After you get a purchase price, **then and only then** do you negotiate your trade. Treat it as two separate transactions in the beginning.

- **Test drive-** While test driving you are checking to see the performance of the car on local streets as well as on the highway. If you have special need such as, car seat or room for products, now is the time to make sure the car is a perfect fit. If you need more than 15 minutes to do a test-drive just let them know. Test the controls inside the car to make sure that you are comfortable driving because this will be your car for a few years. If you can, have a trusted mechanic with you.

Questions to ask a Used Car Dealer

- ☐ **Is the car certified**- ask to see the pre certification inspection. This will tell you what was fixed
- ☐ **How many miles**- calculate the miles by using 15,000 miles per year to date. For example-a 2010 car should have around 105,000 miles (7 years old x 15,000= 105,000)
- ☐ **Does it have a salvage title**- if a car has been in an accident and is declared totaled (a total loss due to accident damage) by an insurance company, it's clean title is replaced with a salvage one. It may be hard to get insurance on a salvage title so check with your insurance company first. i don't recommend buying these type of cars for your first one
- ☐ **Can i see a CARFAX**- check explanation above
- ☐ **How long of a test drive can i take**- check explanation above
- ☐ **Does it come with a warranty**- A warranty is when the manufacturer or seller makes an important promise to stand behind the product. In the case of a car, they agree to cover certain engine parts. The warranty can be for 30 days or sometimes one year, it depends on the manufacturer
- ☐ **What is the cash price**- cash is always King. You can negotiate down at least 5%. Try to convince them that using cash will cut down on paperwork and they will not have to wait for the bank to pay them. Have the cash on hand
- ☐ **What repairs have been made since they purchased it**-did they check the breaks, the oil or do a tune up. This will help you to get a clear picture of what might need to be done. Always get your car serviced when you purchase it by your mechanic.
- ☐ **Do you take trade -ins**- this will help you decide if you want to use your car as part of your down payment.

What is a CARFAX?

A Carfax is a good source when buying a Used Car. A clean report from CarFax just means the vehicle hasn't had any major issues reported. This means the title is clean with no salvage or rebuilt title. It hasn't been involved in flooding or fire, according to records. Here is some information included in a carfax report;

- ☐ Title information
- ☐ vehicle registration
- ☐ odometer reading
- ☐ lemon history
- ☐ accidents
- ☐ vehicle use
- ☐ service and repair maintenance

Basic car maintenance tips

- ☐ **Battery- Maintenance** free and last around 3 years. Sign that it needs to be replace is when you have trouble starting your vehicle
- ☐ **Tires-** inflates to 35 pounds per square inch. Check often and ALWAYS HAVE A GOOD SPARE TIRE

☐ **Engine oil- The LIFE OF YOUR CAR,** check often. Change every 3,000 miles or 3 months

☐ **Transmission fluid- VERY IMPORTANT.** Check every 30,000 miles. Check with the engine running

☐ **Engine coolant-** replace every 30,000 miles or every 2-3 years

☐ **Power steering fluid-** Change every 3 years or 50,000 miles, check frequently

☐ **Brakes and brake fluid-**Check fluid often. When you hear a squealing noise, get your brakes checked

☐ **Air filter-**Change once a year

☐ **Fuel Filter-** Replace annually

☐ **Windshield wipers-**Replace blades every 6-12 months

☐ **Headlights and brake lights-** Walk around your car once a month and check to see if your headlights, blinkers and brake lights are working. To avoid an unnecessary traffic stop you can look at the reflection of the cars behind or infront of you to see if all lights are working properly

☐ **Tune up-** once a year

Get your car serviced before a long trip. If your check engine light is on, get it checked out immediately. It's better to be safe than sorry

Benefits of a AAA membership

Most people have the AAA membership (American Automobile Association). It's a company that offers 24 hour roadside service that protects you anywhere, in any car, whether you are the passenger or driver. There is an annual fee to be a member and different plans. Check AAA.com for other membership benefits. If you have a car, i suggest you purchase one because the price to tow a car without it can be quite expensive

ADVANTAGES OF PUBLIC TRANSPORTATION

Public transportation is a must to any city. Everybody don't drive for different reasons like they are not of age, elderly, sick etc. Here's a snapshot of the advantages of public transportation

☐ **Reduces pollution and road congestion** - the more people who travel by train, tram or bus, the fewer cars on the road.

☐ **Save money-** Travel is cheaper than owning and operating a car.

☐ **Exercise-** Encourages people to have a more active healthy lifestyle, particularly if they are walking or cycling to their station or stop.

☐ **Creates a sense of community.** For example, people traveling together are more likely to feel a community connection than those traveling in a car in isolation.

DISADVANTAGES OF PUBLIC TRANSPORTATION

While public transportation is a great way to save money it can also be stressful. In some communities, routes can be very limited, which can be a major disadvantage for travelers who do not have an alternative means of getting around. Here are some other disadvantages

☐ **Routing-** A lot of stops and limited coverage for certain areas

☐ **Inconvenience-** If the transportation service is late, so are you

☐ **Privacy issues-** Over crowded and no personal space

☐ **germs-** If you are sitting next to a sick person, you may catch their germs

☐ **Threat to personal safety-** is a major concern. Always be aware and alert

Tips on using safe public transportation

☐ **Headphones off-** headphones are dangerous because you are blocking out your surroundings, displaying that you have an electronic device of value, missing announcements and someone could sneak up on you

☐ **Don't speak to strangers-** Sometimes you are targeted if you are a frequent customer and could be putting yourself in danger. Never tell a stranger that you become familiar with your personal information

☐ **Put valuables away-** you will be reducing the chances of getting robbed

☐ **Know the schedule-** this will reduce you from having a long waiting time, especially at night.

☐ **Know playing around-** Use common sense and stay focused

☐ **Be vigilant -** Trust your gut and avoid danger

Purchasing your first car is exciting but it's not all it's cracked up to be. You have to be very responsible and pay attention to your dash board because your car will tell you when there is a problem. Drive safe and no texting while driving, See you on the highway

CHAPTER 16

FOOD AND EXERCISE

Never go food shopping without a list, this will cause you to over spend. Never go food shopping hungry because you will buy everything in the store lol. As a college student, you must learn to eat on a budget, but that does not restrict you only to ramen noodles and peanut butter and jelly. Just focus on the necessary things that you need to eat to survive your early morning rush to class, practice or the library. Your list should consist of cereal, fruit, saltine crackers, nuts, bread and juice. Make sure you have bowls so that you can shop for some of your items from the cafe. Another good source of protein for a college student who is on the run is hot dogs, boiled eggs, oodles and noodles, tuna fish, can vegetables and don't forget Beefaroni

Why use a grocery list?

- ☐ **A grocery list saves you money**-you will do less impulse shopping and have more money for the Needs vs Wants
- ☐ **A grocery list saves you time**- it helps to eliminate mindless wandering and floating through aisles aimlessly.
- ☐ **A grocery list helps with food waste**-Buying more than what is needed, especially food that has to be eaten buy a certain date, will eliminate food spoiling
- ☐ **A grocery list is a tool for meal planning**-you will make healthier food choices for your family and save your waistline, lol

Where to Food Shop for less. Chain stores are great when they have specials but you also need a backup plan. Here are a few tips;

- ☐ **Dollar tree**
- ☐ **Farmers market**
- ☐ **Dollar general**

Essential Items for a Basic Grocery List

Grocery shopping doesn't rate high on the list of fun household chores for most people. However, having a basic grocery list of cheap and healthy foods can make this task a bit easier. If you're trying to cut costs, the following items may be good ones to make staples n your shopping list.

- ☐ **Pasta**: pasta can easily be incorporated in to many nutritious and inexpensive meals. Stock linguine, rotini, penne, and elbow macaroni. The classic college student staples of ramen noodles and macaroni and cheese are also quite cheap, but not healthy enough to eat on a regular basis. Try mixing whole wheat pasta with regular varieties for a more healthy and filling alternative.

- ☐ **Rice**: More than just the basis for many great stir fry dishes, rice is an excellent alternative to pasta. Instead of white rice, however, look for the more nutritious brown rice or wild rice.

- ☐ **Beans**: Beans are a staple in vegetarian diets because they're a great source of protein. Beans and rice may be the classic frugal meal idea, but there are many other recipes to consider as well. Try making a yummy three-bean soup or bean burritos.

- ☐ **Potatoes**: French fries and potato chips aren't healthy, but a bag of regular whole potatoes is both inexpensive and nutritious. Experiment with fun baked potato toppings to make a number of quick and easy meals.

- ☐ **Eggs**: Eggs are a great kitchen staple for someone on a tight budget. You can enjoy scrambled eggs for breakfast or make your own homemade version of McDonald's Egg McMuffin. For lunch, try adding eggs to some fried rice with veggies. Hard-boiled eggs make a simple yet healthy snack.

- ☐ **Pancake mix**: When you're in a hurry, nothing beats a "just add water" pancake mix for a cheap and easy meal. Children especially love the novelty of the occasional "breakfast for dinner" meal.

- ☐ **Tuna**: Tuna salad sandwiches may be the most obvious thing you can think of to do with this cheap grocery staple, but tuna can also be used to add protein to several different pasta and rice dishes.

- ☐ **Ground turkey**: Significantly cheaper than ground beef, ground turkey is also quite low in fat.

- ☐ **Canned or frozen fruits and vegetables**: If you're on a tight budget, or simply don't want to worry about your produce spoiling before you have a chance to eat it, canned or frozen fruits and vegetables are a smart choice

What are coupons?

A coupon is a ticket or document issued by retailers, to be used in retail stores as a part of sales promotions. The average person saves about 12% off there bill by using coupons. Coupons are a great way to save money if you have the time and patience to apply yourself

The Pros

- ☐ **Stock up**- Most items are free or super cheap, so you can purchase more
- ☐ **Price conscious**- couponers do more price comparison because of the deals they can get
- ☐ **Discounts**- coupons sometime offer better discounts than the store sales

The Cons

- ☐ **Time consuming**- you have to organize them and remember to have them with you when you shop
- ☐ **Unhealthy food**- **a lot** of the coupons are for processed food which are not the healthiest items to buy
- ☐ **Longer check out**- People in the checkout line will roll their eyes at you, and your checker might not know the policies, have to call the manager, it takes time, and is pretty embarrassing for you while you wait

Basic cooking techniques

Cooking can be scary if you have never tried it before. I am no gourmet chef, i leave that to my brother Larry (Quan), but i can cook. Here are some basic cooking techniques to get you through your college and young adult days because cooking is definitely a life skill.

- ☐ **Boiling pasta**-Add 2//3 water to a pot, use a teaspoon of salt for every gallon, add pasta to boiling water, let boil for 8-10 minutes, stirring occasionally, taste test and when its done drain it and you are ready to go
- ☐ **Chopping vegetables**- Use a cutting board, wash and dry the vegetables, put them on the cutting board and slice using a downward stroke
- ☐ **Sauteing meat**- place your pan on the stove top using medium to high heat, add enough oil to coat the bottom of the pan, add meat and seasonings, brown on one side and then flip and repeat the same process until your meat is brown. Don't over or under cook

☐ **Scrambling eggs-** place the non stick pan on the stove using medium heat, crack the eggs in a mixing bowl and scramble, add butter to the pan, add eggs, push the eggs around using a folk until done. Don't over cook

☐ **Making a stir fry-** Use a wok or non stick frying pan, get all your ingredients together before you start and make sure you rinse them, use a chopping board to cut your meats and vegetables into bite size pieces, use vegetable or canola oil an turn heat to medium-high, cook meat and remove, cook vegetables about 2 minutes then add meat and little soy sauce, serve with rice. This is a healthy super fast meal

☐ **Using a slow cooker-** Use a Crock Pot for all your slow cooking meals. The beauty of this pot is you can through all of your ingredients in at once, add seasoning and a little water. Slow cook on medium so the meat is not mushy and come home to a great healthy meal later that night.

There are plenty of other methods to use for beginners but i thought that i would share my favorites

Exercise

Exercise is important to your health and well being. Through exercise you will improve your mind, body and soul. Exercise delivers oxygen and nutrients to your tissues and helps your cardiovascular system work more efficiently. When your heart and lung health improve, you have more energy to tackle daily chores. Most people that exercise add years to there life and its a great way to feel better, boost your health and have fun. Here are some benefits of exercising;

☐ **Controls your weight-** When you engage in physical activity, you burn calories. The more intense the activity, the more calories you burn. Consistency is the key.

☐ **Controls health conditions-** Regular exercise helps prevent or manage a wide range of health problems and concerns, including stroke, metabolic syndrome, type 2 diabetes, depression, a number of types of cancer and arthritis. When your blood is flowing smoothly, it decreases your risk of cardiovascular diseases.

- ☐ **Improves your mood-** Having a stressful day or need an emotional boost, working out or going for a walk can help. Physical activity stimulates various brain chemicals that may leave you feeling happier and more relaxed.

- ☐ **Boost energy-** Simple exercise like doing choirs or walking up the stairs instead of taking the elevator makes a difference. Regular physical activity can improve your muscle strength and boost your endurance.

- ☐ **Social-** Physical activity can also help you connect with family and friends in a fun social setting. Joining a dance class, outdoor hiking or bike riding are all ways to meet new people or just have fun with family and friends.

Make exercise a part of your life style, not just another job to do. Eating healthy and exercising is important to keeping your energy level high and it keeps you looking great. We should eat to live, not live to eat.

If you are looking for a chef to cater your entertainment needs or business events email us at MoniqueDonyaleProd@yahoo.com subject-Chef Larry Mckever

CHAPTER 17

HYGIENE TIPS

What is hygiene?

Hygiene is a set of practices performed for the preservation of health. **personal hygiene** is defined as individual practices related to health and cleanliness.

When a young boy or girl starts to mature, many physical changes take place. Some of these changes include an increase in body hair, an increase in sweat (accompanied with body odor), facial skin problems and an oily scalp. Good personal hygiene should be practiced to combat the problems associated with these changes and to avoid contracting any diseases related to poor personal grooming. Use the following personal hygiene tips for adolescents on a day-to-day basis if you are an adolescent who wants to practice good personal hygiene.

Hair Hygiene- Making sure your hair is clean becomes more of a priority when a boy or girl reaches adolescence because the scalp produces more oil at this time. This makes it necessary for the use of a shampoo made for oily hair and more frequent shampooing.

Facial Skin Hygiene-Wash your face two times a day without fail. Adolescents go through a period in which their oil glands produce more oil, and some adolescents wind up with acne. Use skin care products made to treat acne, and if your acne symptoms do not improve after eight weeks, go to a dermatologist to see what he can do to help you.

Avoid using anything on your face that contains oil if you have acne, and do not rub the skin on your face with a heavy hand. Do not spend too much time under the sun, and keep your hands off your face. Go to a licensed esthetician for an acne facial, and ask her to extract blackheads and pimples.

Body Hygiene- Bathe each day with body wash and water to cleanse the sweat from your body. Sweat creates odor, and an adolescent will sweat more because his sweat glands are working more diligently at this time in his life. Sweat will also have a heavier odor in an adolescent. Apply deodorant or antiperspirant to underarms to keep sweating under control and to mask underarm odor if needed.

Body Hair Hygiene-Shave the hair on your face with an electric shaver to look well groomed if you are a guy. Use a nonelectric razor if you do not have an electric shaver, and use a new blade in the razor to avoid cutting your skin. Girls should shave their legs and underarms with an electric razor to avoid cutting themselves.

Oral Hygiene-Use a new, or fairly new toothbrush and toothpaste that contains fluoride with which to brush your teeth after meals, and floss at night. Brushing and flossing may help to prevent bad breath and cavities. Make it a point to practice good oral hygiene every day. Go to the dentist every six months to have your teeth checked and cleaned. See your dentist if you have persistent bad breath.

Vaginal Hygiene-Do not douche often, as doctors do not recommend douching. The vaginal area of the body produces fluids that cleanse the vagina naturally. Wash the pubic area with a mild soap and water to keep the area clean and free of odor. See a gynecologist if you experience abnormal itching, pain, a burning sensation or a yellow/green or lumpy white fluid coming out of your vagina. Make an appointment with your doctor if you experience pain when you urinate.

Navigating the Health Care System

Tips to help you find a good doctor-The list of things to look for in picking a doctor below should be helpful to most anyone in the market for a good doctor. My daughter Champayne experienced this when we moved her to North Hollywood, California in May 2016 to continue her education at New York Film Academy for acting, directing and producing

Decide if you are looking for a primary care doctor or a specialist

- ☐ **Primary care- diagnose and treats a wide range of common illnesses and conditions. They often give patient advice and education on preventing disease and will coordinate or write a referral to a specialist when needed**
- ☐ **Specialist- has advanced training in a certain area of medicine focusing on a particular disease, condition or procedure. Most of the time your primary doctor will give you a referral according to your insurance network so you don't have to pay the cost out of pocket.**

Find out if the doctor is in good standing with State agencies that grant licenses to physicians. Check a website called DocFinder. this site reports whether disciplinary action or criminal charges have been filed against them. State boards are also good in your area. You clearly have to make sure that the doctor you choose is in your network and is a fit with your needs.

Evaluate your Doctor before making a decision. Here are some tips;

- ☐ **Male or female-** It's your choice but your comfort level will help you explain why you are there.
- ☐ **Rapport-** Do you have good chemistry and would you recommend this doctor to someone else
- ☐ **Cleanliness-** Is the office clean, are the people friendly and dressed neat and professional.
- ☐ **Attitude-** Do you feel you like this doctor, does he respect you as a person and does he take you serious

☐ **Availability-** Are they always to busy when you need an appointment, are you always working on their schedule, Do they take time out to answer your questions or just brush you off..

☐ **Organization-** Are they with a group of doctors or by themselves. This maters when it's vacation time because you want to be able to be referred to another doctor in case you have an emergency. Although a solo doctor has other doctors that they can refer you to in these instances

☐ **Age-** Sometime age leans toward the experience level or retirement plans. Some people don't like switching doctors often. The age should not be a deciding factor.

☐ **Reputation-** You can go online and check to see what comments and reviews people are making about your perspective doctor. Bad news travels fast.

Nothing can really give you a feel for whether you've selected the right doctor like an office visit and a face-to-face meeting. Be sure you feel comfortable in the office and with the physician and nurses. Your primary care physician should be someone you trust and can rely on to help manage your health care.

Tips for Finding a Good Dentist

Finding a good dentist is an essential part of having good dental health. If we do not like or do not feel comfortable with our dentist there is a good chance that we will avoid them. Finding a good dentist involves several factors such as the dentist's reputation, their office location, the cleanliness of their office, how they interact with patients and whether or not they are a member of the American Dental Association.

☐ **Dentist's Reputation-**When searching for a dentist as friends, family, co-workers and neighbors about their dentists. Ask them about how they feel about their dentist. Contact the American Dental Association and the Better Business Bureau to research your potential dentist's reputation

- ☐ **Location--**When choosing a dentist make sure that they are located close to your home and/or work. If they are more than thirty minutes away choose another dentist. If you have a dental emergency you want to make sure that you can get to your dentist quickly.

- ☐ **Office Cleanliness-**Take a tour of their office to make sure it is clean and organized. A dirty office may lead to you getting sick when you have work done. If the office isn't organized it could lead to lost files and dental records. A good dentist will take you on a tour and will have a clean and organized office. If the office is a mess there is a chance that the instruments used may not be clean either.

- ☐ **Dentist's Personality-**Your dentist should be friendly and knowledgeable. They should be happy to answer any and all questions and should explain all procedures thoroughly. If your dentist seems like he/she just doesn't want to be there then move on. Dentists who hate their jobs may not be as good at them as dentists who love what they do.

- ☐ **American Dental Association-**Dentists are not required to become a member of this association and not being a member does not mean that they are not good dentists. However, dentists who are a member are required to attend conferences and classes that advance and update their dental skills and education.

Hygiene is very important to your character. Always be aware of your body odor, wash daily and use deodorants and body sprays. Rremember your nose is the closest thing to your mouth so keep your teeth clean to prevent bad breathe.

CHAPTER 18

BEAUTY BUDGET

BUDGETING

A budget is a financial document used to project future income and expenses, a life skill that you need to master. These questions usually help me to stay on track and stay on budget. Before you shop ask yourself these questions?

- ☐ What occasion am i shopping for?
- ☐ What do you wear with frequency?
- ☐ What do you believe you really need?
- ☐ How do you want to be presented?

Essential items every woman should own;

- ☐ **Accessories-** having the right accessories will dress up a plain outfit and make it Fab
- ☐ **Black Dress-** A black dress is always safe especially if you are unsure of the attire for the night
- ☐ **Black Undergarments-** You need black undergarments when wearing white clothes.(please don't wear white on white). Black will help to hide all of your insecurities
- ☐ **Long coat-** long coats are classy and look better when wearing formal clothes
- ☐ **Classic dress pants-** When attending business meetings a pair of dress pants will always be appropriate, but not to tight ladies

- ☐ **Black and White shirt-** These to colors will match with anything, just add a few accessories
- ☐ **Work out clothes-** A must have in your trunk at all times. A good work out in between time will keep your energy up and illness down
- ☐ **Jeans-** A good fitting pair of jeans will always do the job. You can wear them with heels or flats and turn heads
- ☐ **Blazer-** If you are going for the dressy but casual look, then wearing a blazer will give you what you need
- ☐ **Black heals-** Yes black heels will compliment any outfit you wear whether sling backs, block heels or tie up, you will make a statement.
- ☐ **Black Skirt-** This garment will be your magic trick to awesome. You can wear it long or short and it will bring out the classy look in an outfit.

INVESTING IN YOUR WARDROBE

Focus on what you need and what will last for you. Investing in three key areas of your wardrobe, then shopping in stores that carry inexpensive trendy pieces is a great way you can build your wardrobe. One can't have any snobbery about it, there are too many great places to shop that are really affordable now.

Before you hit the stores you should keep three things in mind—silhouette, proportion and fit. "It is essential that we try things on and just say," Gee, it looks great on the rack or it looks great on her—therefore it will translate well on me, this is so not true. Just because they make it in your size does not mean you look good in it.

Here are the four areas of your wardrobe that you should invest in:

- ☐ **A long coat:** A trench coat is the perfect piece of outerwear to invest in. Not like Shaft but more on the classic side. Remember your outer appearance is seen first so make sure you can throw it on over anything and look great.

- ☐ **The sweatsuit alternative:** You need to have something you can wear when traveling or running errands that is comfortable and easy, but looks good. Some jeans and a sweater or nice casual top with some flat trendy boots and a little accessories will always do the trick.

- ☐ **A variety of shoes:** A boot, some heels and a nice pair of loafers are the three types of a shoe wardrobe that every woman should have in her closet. Personally I'm a heels girl, but if you're in college you may prefer a flat shoe.

- ☐ **Undergarments-** woman should buy new undergarments as needed but at least every 3-6 months. You should have multiple pairs of back undergarments because they mesh better with most clothes.

Wardrobe intervention: Ten Tips for Cleaning out the Clutter and Having an Awesome closet

If you've ever spent any time staring at a closet full of clothes while thinking, I have nothing to wear! When you open your closet doors each morning, do you feel a sense of anxiety? If getting dressed in the morning is the most stressful part of your day, then time for you to consider a wardrobe intervention. No matter the shape, size, or layout, the closet should be a place of solace where you can prepare for a productive day at work or a fun night on the town. Clutter can be overwhelming. A packed, unorganized closet forces you to wear the same items over and over—or even worse, clothes that no longer work for you. In the process of cleaning out your closet, you might find you don't need all of the things you own to look good or be happy. Here are ten tips for making over your closet, and in the process, your wardrobe:

Get started by getting rid of the obvious.

- ☐ **To begin your closet clean out, dis guard all clothes that you haven't worn in the past year.** If in doubt, try it on right there on the spot. If it isn't perfect, get rid of it

- ☐ **Picture yourself in a nice outfit**. While you're trying on outfits, visualize your current style, not how you dressed last year. Once you have decided what works together, group these looks by occasion, color and season in your closet. This will make preparing for a night out, office meeting, or vacation a breeze.

- ☐ **Hangers are important**. It's time to let go of those old, cheap wire hangers and invest in some quality ones for your closet. Not only can wire hangers misshape or damage clothing, they also make it easier for clothes to get tangled up with one another or to get lost in your closet. Invest in some good, solid wood or plastic hangers for your closet renovation

- ☐ **You shouldn't reminisce about how you used to look in an outfit**. Be honest with yourself and judge how the outfit looks now, not when (or if) you lose 10 pounds. You'll have the memories those clothes conjure whether those pieces are in your closet or not! Take a picture, they last longer. There's nothing wrong with wearing trendy pieces, as long as you wear them only when they are in style. Holding on to outdated styles creates clutter and increases the risk of a major fashion trap. Get rid of outdated clothing now There's nothing wrong with buying trendy clothes; just be sure you know when the trend is on the way out!

- ☐ **There is nothing wrong with quality instead of quantity.** Do you really need 10 pairs of black pants, or would just one or two great fitting pairs work better in your wardrobe? When you have quality pieces that fit great, you'll find that you won't want to wear the other. Instead, embrace your limited closet space as inspiration to make smarter shopping purchases.

- ☐ **Match your wardrobe to your lifestyle.** Ask yourself: Does my wardrobe match my CURRENT lifestyle? If you're a corporate attorney, then it's reasonable for you to own five black suits. But if you're a cosmetologist working in a salon, it's probably not. And while ten bathing suits aren't necessary for living in New Jersey, they made perfect sense when you lived in Florida. You need to determine the right amount of casual, dress, and party outfits you need based on your lifestyle. If you find yourself avoiding a pair of shoes, either because they're uncomfortable or out of style, it's time to donate or discard them. Let go of how much you paid for them, how great they looked with those jeans you can't fit, that you used to own. If you don't wear them on a regular basis, they are adding to the clutter. It's all about accessibility.

☐ **Keeping key pieces easily accessible.** To start keep the items you wear often at eye level so that you'll be able to find and wear the items that look best on you with ease. Move seasonal items, such as rain boots and heavy winter coats to a hall closet to make room for frequently worn items. And make an effort to rotate the pieces you wear to avoid wearing the same things over and over. After all, you don't want to miss out on wearing that stunning body shaping dress simply because it was stuck in the back corner of your closet!

☐ **Say good-bye to stains.** Be realistic about your ability to salvage stained items: Discard anything with a stain you wish you could remove, but just can't. The same applies for holes, rips and missing buttons. This will make room for presentable items that you'll wear on a weekly basis. Stop trying to make it look like you have more clothes than you really do.

☐ **Don't ostracize your accessories.** Make having a space for accessories a priority when it come to your closet. By banishing your accessories to a remote location away from your closet, you're limiting your ability to utilize these staple pieces daily. Having your accessories in close proximity to your clothes will also make it easier to mix and match different ensembles you may not have considered before.

Secrets of Highly Successful Sale Shoppers. (My daughter Champayne and I live by these rules, lol)

- ☐ **Buy off season-** All fashionistas know that you buy a bathing suit in December and sweater in August to get the best sale prices. You may miss out on the latest fashion but you can always dress up your outfit with good accessories and a banging hair style. Remember if you are by coastal that garment is in season somewhere..
- ☐ **Learn sales lingo-** learn your stores routine, when they start moving items to the back it's because that's when they will start doing the mark downs as low as 70% off and you can dive right in and shop shop, shop
- ☐ **Invest in classics-**These items never go out of style. Trends have a short life cycle so be careful so your wardrobe don't look outdated
- ☐ **Mix and match-** Don't always buy matching outfits, you get more looks when you have clothes that you can match with other clothes. A good example is jeans, blazers, black shirts and more
- ☐ **Beware of buying recklessly-** just because a designer shirt is on sale for 70% off and you don't have a need for it or you don't LOVE IT, then don't buy it. You will be wasting your money because you will never wear it.

☐ **Buy @ boutiques-** Explore your fabulocity by shopping at a boutique. They offer a lot of one of a kind items that you will love. On line boutiques offers a quaint and unique style of clothes that you may not find in your local retain stores.

Shop at MoniqueDonyaleCollection.com

How to wash your clothes

The proper care of your clothes is just as important as buying them. This is a very important life skill. Not knowing how to wash and dry your clothes can be very expensive if you start ruining them. Here are some tips on how to wash your clothes;

☐ **Select soiled clothes and report to the laundry area**
☐ **Sort them by color into piles-** usually you will have 3 piles(white, light and dark) wash your towels and sheets separately.
☐ **Each pile is it's own load**
☐ **Load the machine-** When washing light and dark clothes just use detergent, no bleach. Only use the bleach in the white clothes
☐ **Understand the knobs-** Wash light colors in warm water, dark colors in cold water and white colors in hot water
☐ **Close the door and let them wash-** Usually about 30 minutes
☐ **Return when the machine stops and place them in the dryer or hang dry-** put one load in the dryer at a time

Tips

☐ Don't leave your clothes wet in your washer for more than 24 hours, they will get musty and moldy.
☐ The recommended detergent amounts are about twice what you need (unless you have hard water, in which case, you may need more). Use half of what they recommend & your clothes will be just as clean and your detergent will last twice as long.
☐ Take the sheets off the bed, wash them and put them right back on. Less time will be spent folding/storing.

- ☐ Over drying wears fabric out faster; try to leave a little moisture in (not too much though), it will dry before you get to using it anyway.
- ☐ If your dryer is near the shower, pull towels/clothes directly from the dryer if they are in there, hence less folding.
- ☐ Have hooks in your closet for your favorite pants and shirts that you wear constantly, don't fold and store them, just hang them up.
- ☐ If you're sharing an apartment or living with people you know, it sometimes helps to join in the washing, especially the case with reds, as many people don't have a full load of red clothes in their wardrobe. Doing laundry together saves money and time, and lowers your impact on the environment.
- ☐ For anyone who uses one-colored socks or dress socks: when you are low on socks, give what remains to Goodwill and buy like 30 pairs all same style of black. No more sorting.
- ☐ Fold as little as possible. Just stack your washcloths like pancakes.
- ☐ never forget to separate clothes before washing. Clothes can change color if you wash reds and whites together.

When shopping for the latest outfits but sticking to a budget, you can always shop on line at our boutique MoniqueDonyaleCollection.com Chammy will keep your NY, NJ and LA LOOK POPPING

CHAPTER 19

MENTORS AND SPIRITUAL ADVISERS

What is a career mentor?

A career mentor is usually someone in your company or similar field who has more experience or someone you have worked with in the past and still share a cordial relationship. They take on the role as a counselor, motivator and a guiding force in your career. They will give you impartial advice as well as coach an guide you. You should feel comfortable talking to them and speaking your mind

How to find a career mentor

Traditionally a mentor can not be purchased and does not require a monetary exchange. Your relationship with your mentor will come from life lessons and experiences that money can't buy. Look for these qualities

☐ **Clues of success**- Someone higher in the company or business in the similar line of work who live to work, not work to live. Successful people are successful for a reason. People who have achieved greatness in an area of their lives are typically using great strategies. And these people tend to make excellent mentors. Start to look for people around you who exemplify the skills you want to acquire.

☐ **Someone you admire**- Someone you have high value and respect for. They are motivating and compassionate about that business.

You should also share some of the same values and work ethics. To be sustainable and healthy, mentoring must be a two-way street. Both parties need to give 110% to the relationship. This ensures that the mentor and mentee continually learn from each other. Seek out ways to add value to their life as well. Understand what matters most to them and find ways to contribute.

TIPS

- ☐ A manager is not a good mentor, while you are working toward the same interest, you just have different goals
- ☐ Do need choose a direct competitor that is on your level because it may be a conflict of interest.

Use different mentors for different faucets of your life. If you want to know about being a good mom, then look for a good mom and ask for her wisdom

Who can benefit from a Spiritual Adviser

Anybody who want to seek it. A Spiritual Adviser will enhance the quality of one's life on a SPIRITUAL LEVEL. After going through challenges and life struggles and facing each of them, I came to realize that each life event was a Blessing in Disguise. Every time a door closed, a window opened. Each event, no matter how hard it was, led me to grow spiritually and led me to walk on the spiritual path to Heal. Prophet Beaty is my spiritual adviser and I thank God for him. A **Spiritual Advisers** role is to serve you and guide you so that you can learn HOW TO HEAL YOURSELF.

Here are some signs that may indicate you are a good candidate for Spiritual Advising

- ☐ No Motivation
- ☐ Lack of Passion in life
- ☐ Feeling stuck
- ☐ Lack of Concentration
- ☐ No Satisfaction in life

- ☐ Having discomfort without a specific reason
- ☐ Low Energy
- ☐ Frequent Injuries
- ☐ Recurring Life Patterns
- ☐ Extreme Fear, Phobia, Obsessive Compulsive Disorder, etc.

Don't be so hard on yourself. Take some time and space whenever you have a set back. What don't kill you, will only make you stronger.

MIND vs BODY

Your MIND can be saying 'I want this' and 'I want that'. That's okay, whoever, sooner or later, you may run into a wall and you tend to get stuck no matter what you try to do as long as you are following what your MIND keeps telling you.... At that point, I highly suggest finding out what your BODY is actually telling you. You may be surprised to find out how twisted your MIND can be towards **Inner and Divine Guidance**.

This twisted mind can be reflected in Relationship issues (such as controlling issue, passive-aggressive syndrome, etc.), it can be reflected on the physical level as a block such as pain, discomfort, sickness, it can be reflected as obstacles in life (injuries, accidents, etc.) and/or it can be reflected in Emotional and Mental states such as Anxiety, Panic Attack, Depression, Mental/Nervous Breakdown, Manic/Bi-Polar disorder, etc.

You may be TRYING TOO HARD??? If that's the case, your MIND needs to SURRENDER........ That's when you may be able to promote HEALING on the Spiritual level.

CONSCIOUSNESS-BASED SPIRITUAL HEALING

Everything manifests because of consciousness. What manifested on the physical, mental and emotional levels is based on CONSCIOUSNESS. What it means is that SHIFT IN CONSCIOUSNESS can promote TRUE HEALING of Body-Mind-Soul. As long as we are dealing with EFFECT on the consciousness, it's like putting band aids over the wounds, but dealing with the CAUSE is getting down to the root of the problem.

Having one or both of these advisers in your life can help to provide a much needed navigational system in your life. Stand for something or fall for anything.....If you would like to call my spiritual adviser Prophet Beatty, he can be reached by email at gregbeatty59@gmail.com or cell 908-664-3335

CHAPTER 20

EMPOWERING PARENTS

Parental advice

While they are trying to finish school, working and deciding their own life plan, they are finding it necessary to lean on us - their parents. Today's realities have made it necessary for parents to muster up a little extra patience and realize their importance in the way of support and encouragement. Parents' attitudes can be a great source of motivation and encouragement as young adult children try to reach a point of separation from them. Most young people do NOT want to live in their parents' homes any longer than necessary. They long for the day when they can be independent of their parents' financial (and other) support and stand on their own two feet. Ultimately, they want to make us, as well as themselves proud.

From my own personal experience, here are some tips and suggestions to guide parents of young adult children who are still living at home. After all, what goes around, comes around, as the old saying goes. There will most likely come a day that we will need THEM to encourage and support US! Young adult children will surely remember the patience, understanding, concern and kindness we have given them and return it ten-fold.

☐ **Let Love Be Your Guide-**Maybe your son stands a foot taller than you now, or your daughter's makeup and wardrobe collections seem to be her biggest interest but they are still your prides and joys! They might LOOK all grown up but they are still struggling to grow and separate from you to lead lives of their own. Remember that even though they don't require as much from you, physically, they still need to know that you love them and support their efforts to grow up and get out on their own.

☐ **Don't Quit Parenting Too Soon**-Many people think that raising a child ends when they turn 18 years old. Not so! A parent's job is never done, no matter how old they are. Yes, you are now in a new phase of their lives - one in which teaching new skills has been lessened. Now is the time to reinforce many things that you have spent many years teaching them such as honesty, integrity, work ethic, goal setting and self-confidence. Your parenting duties now take on a different roll but your presence is greatly important!

☐ **Be There for Them**-Even though we are all busy with our own jobs, commitments and chores, parents of adult children (over 18) need to let them know that we are there for them when they need us. Their needs are much different than they were as young kids. We are no longer changing diapers or carpooling them to their various functions. They are no longer making crayon drawings for us with colorful messages like 'I Love You.' Do not misinterpret this change of 'seasons' with them. They DO love us but are caught up in trying to become independent of us now. They have different worries and concerns that aren't always easy to tap into unless you make yourself available to them. This is easily done by scheduling times to talk regularly with them. Initiate conversations at any time when the opportunity presents itself or decide upon a scheduled time to talk that will work best for both of you. Of course this will be different for each family, depending on their time demands and schedules.

☐ **Listen**-This is a hard one sometimes but a most necessary step to a good relationship with your young adult children. Even though we may think they are being ridiculous at times, we need to be non-judgmental and realize that this 'thing' they are concerned about is real to them. Stress and worries are different for all of us depending on what is going on in our lives. Help your young adult child learn to address and face their fears and worries. Offer healthy advice on how they might be able to change the way they feel and be more in control of their future experiences. Sharing similar instances from your own life is a valuable tool, as well. The more you listen the more you will learn and be better able to be a support system for them.

☐ **Talk About Goal Setting**-By now, your young adult children surely have some idea of what kind of life they would love to have. Many of them have since began baby steps towards those goals as well. That is a good thing! Setting goals that are realistic and reachable is very important in order to maintain momentum. Although it is important to always keep that BIG goal in sight, it is equally important to set smaller goals along the way. As an example, if your child is enrolled in college courses, the completion of each semester is a smaller goal within the bigger one of obtaining a degree! Point these things out to your young adult children so that they can be made to take notice of their ongoing success in reaching their goals!

☐ **Mistakes teach life lessons**-We were all young once and most of us have made many mistakes that we'd much rather forget about than remember. If we look back, we can now see that some of those mistakes taught us some big and rich life lessons. Isn't your adult child worthy of that same learning experience? Bottom line is that they WILL make mistakes and it's okay. Don't expect your young adult child to be perfect. No one is or ever has been - not even you!

☐ **Instill that hard work pays off**-You've probably been doing this for years, but keep on going! Your young adult child may need to hear you say that you are sure they can do whatever it is they have to do along the way. Knowing (and hearing) that you believe in them has value beyond what words can express. It will give them an extra boost of confidence to go to that big job interview, try out for that modeling and acting agency.....or take that dreaded final exam at school. Occasionally mention to them how proud you are of their efforts. Remind that hard work pays off. These kinds of comments will stick with them throughout their lives, so be free (but honest) with them if that is what you feel.

☐ **Take Note of Accomplishments**-Any and all accomplishments made by your young adult child deserve notice! Excessive praise is not what we are looking for here. But by taking a moment to verbally congratulate them on their accomplishment is another way to positively reinforce to them that their efforts have been good enough to warrant your compliment. I've found that an extra smile goes across my kids' faces if they happen to overhear me telling someone else about one of their recent accomplishments! Doesn't everyone like to hear something good about themselves??

☐ **Reinforce the Value of a Higher Education-**Most young adult children are juggling a lot in their daily lives. They are working part time jobs, socializing as well as taking classes for college credits or going to a trade school. Along the way they can begin feeling like it isn't mattering - they aren't looking at the big picture. This is a good time to reinforce to them that what they are doing/ learning in their classes IS valuable towards their future! Each and every credit that is earned is taking them one step closer to their goal of a college degree or being an entrepreneur! Remind them that their continued education will set them apart from those who never bothered taking time for learning. What they learn will be theirs to keep forever and will also speak volumes about them to a potential employer or starting their own business.

☐ **Expect Them To Contribute to the Home Environment-**This all important step will assure that everyone else in the household will maintain their sanity and serenity. Setting ground rules and laying out basic expectations is a necessary step in helping your young adult child learn to respect others. Unless they are paying all of your bills and expenses, they have no right to expect everyone else to succumb to their way of living. Respect is the key here. The world is full of rules and guidelines for us ALL to follow so why not start here in teaching them to act like an adult and be considerate of others' feelings. A little bit of consideration goes a long way in upholding family peace. Also, if your young adult child is able, it is a good idea to expect them to pay a reasonable amount of money as 'rent or household contributions.' After all, life is not free for any adult. This will teach them responsibility and how to pay bills on time. If you feel guilty about doing this, remember it's not about the money as much as it is about teaching them to respect life and its RULES. Life waits for no one to catch up.

156

- ☐ **Keep Teaching the Value of Paying yourself first**-Saving for that proverbial 'rainy day' is an important way we can all invest in our futures. Always take a percentage out of every pay check and PAY YOURSELF FIRST which means save(review finance chapter). This is a great time to keep teaching the value of money. A young adult child can easily capitalize on their 'free ride' and come to realize how much disposable income they have by living with you. That is why giving them some financial responsibilities carries a lot of weight at this time. Sit down together to decide on the amount of money (or percentage of their income) they are planning on putting away in a bank account, then reinvest it into a money marketing account etc. They may argue at first that they don't make enough money to save any. That is not true. Even a little saved is better than none. It might inspire them to save more if they set a goal as to what they are saving for! Maybe a new car could be in their future - or enough money to move out of the home when they are ready could be gathered in this way.

- ☐ **Be Respectful**-If you give respect, you will get it back. Everyone deserves to be treated with respect - even your young adult children. Remain calm, fight fair and remember that you are the parent in this situation and should lead by your example as to how problems, worries, stresses and fear can be addressed and solved.

- ☐ **Let There Be Consequences**-This step requires parents to continue with what they have been doing all along. Bad behavior, especially that of the repeated variety, deserves consequences. This is true for all of us, really, so it needs to be a part of your relationship with your young adult child living in your home. If they do not respect your home or you, you need to be clear that it is not acceptable to you and sit down with them and brainstorm a realistic consequence together.

- ☐ **Be Positive and never stop believing in them**-it won't be long until your young adult child is out living their life away from home. Make the best of this ever changing time with them and remain positive. Good things do happen to good people and they WILL happen to your awesome young adult child. They (as well as you) should expect good things and be open and honest with each other. Always remind them to set realistic goals and believe that they will succeed!

If your young adults would like to still reside at home after the age of 18, you need to Create a "This is still my house Contract", to help set agreements. This needs to be a face to face sit down with everyone involved

THE BREAKDOWN

- ☐ **Visitors-** Be clear with your young adult whether guest are aloud in there room or not. Definetly discuss if overnight guest of a person they are in a relationship with is except able. Never demote your standards to appease them. You are there parent, not there friend.
- ☐ **Conduct-**Discuss how late guest can stay, the noise level and if they can have parties in your home. Let them know if alcohol, drugs and other recreational socializing is except able by them or there guest..
- ☐ **Rent-** Charge your young adult (est. 23 & over) rent to live at home, especially if they are not in grad school. It's not about you needing the money, it's about responsibility and team work. You cannot live anywhere for free, including your house.
- ☐ **Chores-**Discuss what is expected as far as choirs are concerned and what day you would like them done on. They are no better than you and must chip in to keep the house organized. No excuses
- ☐ **Deadlines-**Be clear about the living arrangement time line. Set a goal of when they should be moving out and getting there own place. It doesn't matter if it's 2 years from now, you should always be working toward a goal in life to better your situation.

Plus, special circumstances, contracts for...

- ☐ Adult children who come home with **children of their own.**
- ☐ Grown kids who are home dealing with **drug or alcohol addictions.**

How to enforce the rules of the house with older kids;

They are adults, not children. The same rules you enforced there entire life should stay in effect. The same rules when it came to values, structure, drugs, alcohol and staying out all night should be reiterated. Especially if you have younger kids because you don't want to create a double standard.

As a young adult they should have a little more Independence when staying at home but they have to earn it. If they are in college or trade school, at some point (once they get adapted to there new life) find a part time job. This will give them a sense of moving up in life and building. It makes them feel more responsible and independent. Supporting your kids financially while they are in college (18-23) is a pretty good range. On the other hand if they didn't do good in high school and don't want to go to college or trade school, then they need to get a job at McDonald's or 7 eleven as long as they are working. If they think those jobs are beneath them then they have a THINKING ERROR and it is not except able to you as there parent. Don't blame yourself for your child misconducts in high school or bad behavior that is leading them to this type of work. The **worst thing you could do is be an ENABLER**

Do your kids have a THINKING ERROR?

This will develop around their mid teens. **Your child will start to misread life's problems and come out with the wrong solutions. They** will start to see themselves as victims. For example, they may say "It's not my fault if they didn't finish their choirs or homework or I couldn't help it if they missed curfew. They will become master manipulators if you let them. What your response should be is to teach them time management and consequences for there actions. Don't let them convince you that your crazy and an unfit parent. Stand your ground and be honest with your kids.

Parents for life

As a parent we know that life is not easy. Everything don't always go as planned but you have to have a plan in order to know that. Some people where teen moms and dads, lost your parents at a young age or high school drop outs, but you still made it. You must expect the same energy and ambition from your kids. Don't let them use your fears and guilt of always working to keep food on the table as there reason for not using there 18 years of experience in this world to there advantage. They may have to come back home as an adult but that's okay because we fall down but we get up. I call kids that keep returning home Boomerang kids(a term I once hurd used in conversation and it stuck with me). The bottom line is once you're a parent, you are a parent for life.

Accountability or Tough Love

What parent or family member wants to be supporting 24-30 year old kids? It's one thing for a young adult to be looking as hard as he or she can to find work, to volunteer, or to gain skills or certification needed for employment, but it's an entirely different thing to be living off other folks or the system--sleeping in past noon and partying at leisure.

To be actively looking for work takes as much or more effort, than it takes to actually do a job. It might take 200 applications and 30 interviews to land a job, but doing the preparation usually lands a job. Not doing it, perpetuates joblessness and dependence.

There may come a day when a parent must say, "I'm sorry. There's no more money." If the parent has given fair warning of 3-6 months, has offered advice and financial support to go with that advice, but the young adult has not been accountable, then the parent should not feel guilt when tough love is required.

Sometimes lack of accountability on the part of an adult child has nothing to do with the job market or lack of employable skills. It may actually have more to do with an addiction that could be robbing the adult child of motivation, opportunity, and freedom.

Tough love hurts the parent as much or more than the child. Parents want to give to their kids--even though kids may not always show gratitude, express thanks, or use the gift wisely. It's the nature of a parent to be giving. But there comes a day when a baby bird gets too big for the nest. If it won't take off on its own, the bird may have to be bumped out of the nest to face decision. It will need to choose flight or risk falling. Chances are the bird will fly--but if not, that bird will get one big wake up call and some much needed motivation.

ARE YOU BEING ABUSED BY YOUR ADULT CHILD

Parent Abuse is a form of domestic abuse and is a serious problem which results in physical harm, depression, damage to property, job loss, and family breakdown. It is usually perpetrated by a child in their teens displaying the following behavior towards you and members of your family. It's a growing problem for parents who share their home with abusive young people and there is virtually no support.... Signs include:

- ☐ Afraid of your child
- ☐ they hit you
- ☐ blames you for all of there problems in life
- ☐ intimidates you
- ☐ humiliates you in front off people
- ☐ puts you down and talks about your appearance
- ☐ can't talk on the phone around them
- ☐ you want to call 911 and have them arrested
- ☐ Steals money and property from you
- ☐ blackmails you
- ☐ excessive drug and alcohol usage and profanity toward you

Solution

If you are suffering from Parent Abuse you must recognize that you are not at fault and do not deserve this, as with any form of abuse. Speak to a friend or family member or contact a domestic abuse support group. Seek professional help. Don't let anybody, including your kids take away yourself worth. You must practice self love and demand to be treated with respect.

BE A POWERFUL PARENT AND LEAN ON FAMILY

What your adult children do is not about you. We are responsible for our children as they grow and mature. What they will do with their lives and the good or not so good things they experienced is up to them. Don't be held hostage by feeling you are responsible for another life. It is enough to be responsible for your own.

For more information on being a Powerful Parent email Rochelle V Gray at Empoweryouthplus@gmail.com EmpowerTheYouth.co

CHAPTER 21

THE POWER OF "I AM"

How to be a winner

People who get what they want tend to be the ones who make the effort to *know* what they want. Complaining is easy, even fun, and compared with the challenge of creating a plan for positive change. I gain huge respect for anyone who pushes beyond turbulence and into clarity.

People complain in rich detail about the things that are wrong with their lives: demanding children, overbearing bosses, unprofitable business, and layoffs. But when it comes to specifying the Plan of Action, people become victims. "I just want love," they say. "Passion" And "Inner peace." It's like telling a waiter, "Bring me something delicious. I have no idea what, but I'll know it when I taste it." No order that broad is likely to produce a satisfying result.

Here's the truth: People who get what they want tend to be the ones who make the effort to *know* what they want and put a plan of execution in motion. Nobody said that the road would be easy, but I don't think God brought you this far to leave you. If you'd like your life to vastly improve, you might want to do the same.

Engage in SELF- DISCOVERY

- ☐ A unique approach to engaging in self-discovery, purpose, and fulfillment
- ☐ A positive set of tools to feel more empowered, satisfied, peaceful, and balanced in one's personal and professional life
- ☐ Not therapy, but nonetheless therapeutic, as it enables individuals to look inward, grow, and gain awareness about themselves and what they want
- ☐ A way to go from functional to optimal
- ☐ Through empowering questions, guided visualization, and core energy techniques, you gain greater awareness of your desires, discover blocks that might be stopping you from reaching your goals, and establish new 'rules' about your life, so that you connect inner desires to outer goals.

Understanding What You Want:

Understand that the quickest way to a rich life is to want less. Think carefully about what you REALLY want, then ask yourself is it worth the time, is it worth the sacrifice and will it make you happier? Are you sure? Happiness comes from within and from how you view the world you find yourself in. You can either change the situation you are in, or change the way you feel about it; those are always your only two choice.

Attract the life that you want

In the beginning life is something that you write as you go along until you learn that goal setting will put you on a path to success. Our habits define our destiny. We are always attracting into our lives what we need for our spiritual growth. The game of life requires wisdom, determination and Prayer. So the question is, what do we need to attract more into our lives of what we want? Here are a few tips toward spiritual attraction;

☐ **Make meaningful choices-** Stop making life long choices off of self-serving ego-dominant decisions. Follow your heart, Your heart is tender, kind and guided by meaningful choices.

☐ **Rebuke fear-** Fear doesn't reside in the soul. The soul gives you a calling and it's your unique signature and essence. Fear is not of prayer. You can't Pray and worry.

☐ **Manage your life-** Don't get stuck on the small things. Focus on what's really important and how you can get what you want out of life. Manage your life effectively by organizing your dreams into bite-size chunks, then tap into your divine purpose

☐ **Develop Passion-** Develop passion for who you are and what you are here to contribute. Connect emotionally with what you want to achieve. Successful people develop methods to harness their emotions and focus on who they see themselves being.

☐ **Align to your truth-** Be aware of negative people (i call them dream stealers), there job is to wear you down. See yourself as one with your goal, and the goal as already achieved. Create the emotion of achievement, and use it to inspire you and push forward.

☐ **Follow your intuition-** Don't look in your rear view mirror. People are behind you and in front of you for a reason. The more you use your intuition (you inner self), the more you build trust in your intuitive insight.

☐ **Use Affirmations-** Affirmations harness positive thinking. The mind is a powerful asset that needs plenty of sleep to clear away clutter. Clear the mind through cleansing meditation and quiet time.

☐ **Believe in yourself-** You are something of real value and you have something unique to offer the world. Don't let negative, jealous, lazy individuals direct your steps into misery because misery loves company. When people say to you, "You're doing to much", that simply means that they need to catch up and you need to surround yourself with a more productive circle.

- ☐ **Take Action-** Momentum comes through actions, so do something that moves you forwards. Even a small act is significant. Actions also contain the symbolic power to dissolve fears and build self-confidence and belief.
- ☐ **Prayer-** Speak your life into existence. What God has for you, is for you. The final step is to let go of the outcome and have faith. Sometimes all you need is a little faith. A prayer may be the only thing missing. Develop patience, let go and LET GOD.

"THE POWER OF "I AM"

Finding your divine purpose

Your divine purpose is within you. You don't need to go out into the world to find what it is. You will need to do that in order to follow that purpose, but to find it, all you need to do is ask yourself what you love to do and how you can serve others with that talent. I hate to be the bearer of bad news but in order to find your divine purpose you have to think. Your mind is capable of giving you all the answers you need. Here are a few tips to help you find your divine purpose.

☐ **Meditation**- Before you get out of bed everyday ask yourself, "How can i serve"? Connect with your true essence. Remind yourself that your existence is important and you are in this world to serve a purpose because God don't make no junk. Your mission is to be all you can be and service your fellow human beings because you are not here by accident.

☐ **Passion**- Focus on what you love to do. Think about it, it only matters that you love to do it more than anything, that when you do it, you feel alive like you've never felt before. It doesn't matter what it is as long as it is that special thing to you.

☐ **Serve others**- Tie Serving others into the Passion that you have and find a way to improve the quality of other people's lives by doing it. You have to add value to other people's lives. Use your mind. You should always find self satisfaction in helping others.

☐ **Earn a living doing what you love**- Think about things you can do associated to your passion that will give people what they need or solve a problem that many people have. If you can find a way to give people what they need, you will have no problem turning your purpose into a business that will support you and your love one for a lifetime.

☐ **Check in with your feelings**-Does it make you feel great? Does it make you excited to get up in the morning, like you can't wait to greet the coming day to see what's in store? If you're not feeling this kind of passion about what you're doing, you need to re-think what's actually most important to you.

Your Divine Purpose is different from setting a goal. A goal is a tangible desire with an end result but your Divine Purpose is a way of living. You will be working and growing with your Divine Purpose for the rest of your life. For example your goal may be to go to school and get your Cosmetology license but your Divine Purpose is to self empower people through beauty. You are framing your life with meaning. This is an important step in your spiritual development to prove to yourself that you have the power to affect change and live a well balanced life.

On this journey called life, you will require additional guidance and support in order to be successful during this exciting but challenging time. Life Skills is tied into your Divine Purpose. What you stand for, what you believe in, the lessons you will learn and the life style that you live will be based on your life mission. Be strong, demand respect, stay focused, set goals, reach for the sky and you will fall among the stars. I hope my book "Forgotten Pieces" will help trigger your inner Soul to find peace and your Divine Purpose through Life Skills. See you at the top!!!!!!!

THE END

Printed in the United States
By Bookmasters